Colorful
Personalities

Also by George Boelcke:

The Colors of Leadership and Management

The Colors of Parent & Child Dynamics

The Colors of Relationships

The Stories of Colors

The Colors of Customers and Sales

Keeping Your Money

It's Your Money! Tools, tips & tricks to borrow smarter
and pay it off quicker (Canadian Edition)

It's Your Money! Tools, tips & tricks to borrow smarter
and pay it off quicker (U.S. Edition)

*A practical, fun and powerful guide to understanding
the four Colors, which will change your life,
relationships and the way you look at others*

Colorful
Personalities

Discover your personality type
through the power of Colors

George J. Boelcke, F.C.I.

With your own
personality
assessment

Vantage Publishing
U.S. office: 1183-14781 Memorial Dr. Houston, TX 77079
Canadian office: Box 4080, Edmonton, AB T6E 4S8
E-mail: sales@vantageseminars.com
Web-site: www.vantageseminars.com

Library and Archives Canada Cataloguing in Publication

Boelcke, George J., 1959-
        Colorful Personalities: discover your personality type through the power of colors / George J. Boelcke. – 2nd ed.

Includes index.
ISBN 0-9736668-1-1

        1. Typology (Psychology) 2. Color—Psychological aspects. I. Title.

BF698.3.B63 2005   155.2'64   C2005-900233-6

Design & artwork assistance: David Macpherson
Edited by: Veniece Tedeschini, Calgary
Layout & typeset by: Ingenieuse Productions, Edmonton

Colorful Personalities is a registered trademark of Vantage Consulting

Printed and bound in the United States of America

This book is dedicated as a thank you, first and foremost, to the thousands of people from all walks of life who have attended so many of my seminars. To this day, there still isn't a session that is exactly the same as another.

To Thelma Box, whose incredible Choices Seminar (choicesintl.com) first introduced me to the power of Colors, and unknowingly, is one of the biggest role models in my life – as anyone would be who continuously challenges others to keep dreaming, following their passions, and living their purpose.

To Ann Zitaruk – one of the few friends a Gold person needs. For her insightful feedback and her unwavering support, in so many ways, to continue my "Be-Do-Have."

Contents

The Colors Self-Assessment

Welcome to your journey of discovery! This is a journey of learning many tools and insights to understanding and appreciating each other. One of celebrating our differences and of discovering a new set of glasses through which we see, and interact with, each other.

On the next two pages is a short assessment. There is also an extra copy at the end of the book. It is important to remember that this is a self-assessment and not a test. There are no right or wrong answers; just groups of words designed to identify your own preferences, values and priorities. It is not about how others would describe you, or how you might act in any specific situations, but rather how you see yourself overall. It is also not a quiz that is designed to label or stereotype you, or anyone else. That would be as wrong and inaccurate as it would be pointless.

When you have completed the assessment, you will have a score in each of the different Color groups. Your highest score will likely best describe the largest part of your personality. You may also discover that the detailed sections of each chapter describe you more accurately than the assessment.

We are all a combination of the four personality parts, or Colors. These four parts of our personality are like pieces of a jigsaw puzzle, and each of these four has to be present to make a complete person. What make us unique are the different sizes of these pieces. Some will have all four in balance, while others can have one or two much larger than others. There is no better or worse – only different, as each Color is equally valuable, special and important. Or in the words of the Billy Joel song: "I love you just the way you are."

Let the journey begin...

The Colors Self-Assessment

Score each group of words, for all eight questions, on a scale of:

      4 – which is the most like you

      3 – which is quite a bit like you

      2 – which is a little bit like you

      1 – which is the least like you

(Each question can have only one score of 1, one 2, one 3 and one 4)

1. a) ____ compassion, sharing, sympathetic

    b) ____ duty, detailed, traditions

    c) ____ verbal, risk-taker, promoter

    d) ____ rational, knowledge, visionary

2. a) ____ feelings, meaningful, cooperation

    b) ____ conservative, reliable, stability

    c) ____ spontaneous, generous, action

    d) ____ credibility, focused, probing

3. a) ____ authentic, encouraging, spiritual

    b) ____ devoted, cautious, status-quo

    c) ____ surprises, freedom, short-cuts

    d) ____ inventive, principled, competence

4. a) ____ unique, sensitive, peace-maker

    b) ____ steady, planning, loyal

    c) ____ open-minded, playful, hands-on

    d) ____ curious, determined, rational

5. a) ____ tender, involved, connecting
   b) ____ lists, procedural, responsible
   c) ____ competitive, outgoing, direct
   d) ____ exploring, skeptical, complex

6. a) ____ devoted, caring, self-improvement
   b) ____ dependable, structured, belonging
   c) ____ flexible, daring, persuasive
   d) ____ independent, perfectionist, reserved

7. a) ____ intuition, sharing, positive
   b) ____ orderly, honor, rule-follower
   c) ____ immediate, skillful, active
   d) ____ theoretical, calm & cool, learning

8. a) ____ affectionate, accommodating, harmony
   b) ____ private, serious, moral
   c) ____ networking, adventure, winning
   d) ____ analytical, logical, improving

Your total score for:

a) Blue ____   b) Gold ____   c) Orange ____   d) Green ____

(The total of your four scores will equal 80)

Chapter 1

Introduction

"We meet ourselves time and again in a thousand disguises on the path of life." Carl Jung

Most self-help books are geared toward teaching us to become better at one thing or another. Most of us already understand what some of our challenges are, but how much time should we spend becoming good at something we're not? Would it be better, perhaps, to understand what we are like, celebrate our strengths and appreciate our differences? Can we learn to write with our other hand? Yes, of course – but it will never really be comfortable, will it? Just like changing the hand we write with, many attempts to change parts of our personality will also meet with limited success.

Instead, take some time to celebrate your strengths and joys. Look at those many things that make you a great friend, parent, partner, and individual. Discovering your Colors results in many "Ah ha!" moments. It creates and strengthens the understanding of who you really are when you look in the mirror and when others see you. It will put words to many feelings and stresses, and will help you celebrate your uniqueness and special talents. You will discover the road map of where you are, and the tools for discovering where your journey can take you.

"I see your true colors shining through.
So don't be afraid to let them show – a beautiful you."
Phil Collins

Let's face it, life would be much easier if we each came with a label describing our personality type, or perhaps some form of instruction manual for each unique personality. Unfortunately, we don't come with such a manual or label. We don't even come with the same list of likes and dislikes, stresses or strengths.

However, we can easily discover many common traits about each other without too much difficulty. All that's required is an open mind, the desire to find value in others, and the willingness to look beyond our judgments.

The first step in any journey of growth always starts at the place we are currently at. After all, it is only useful to know where you're going if you know the place from which you're starting. Perhaps it is time to first take a step back, to find that point on the map where you're at right now and to gain an understanding of the long list of special traits that makes you just the way you are. To define your special strengths, stresses, and the many things that you already know how to do without any effort, practice, or help from a book. You cannot become a different person than you are. Besides being impossible, it it also not necessary.

That list should also include the things that cause you stress, annoy you, or often cause tensions. There is an old saying, "You don't know what you don't know." Perhaps it is time to discover, or really define, what you're like and what makes you tick.

It needs to be made clear that personality types, and the study of human behavior, is not an exact science. We are always limited to general preferences and common denominators. Throughout the book are the words *majority, often, tend to, prefer, largely,* and so on, to clearly emphasize that the study and understanding of human behaviors is not easy. It never has been, and never will be. Clearly defined black or white answers cannot be used in human interactions, or in understanding each other. They are never right or wrong, but always different and unique. Everyone's individual personality is what makes them, each family unit, every community and workplace, different and special.

Psychological types are also never designed to stereotype or pigeonhole. They do not put people into categories or label them. That would be as wrong as it would be pointless. It does, however, supply a basic outline of personality types and preferences. To that end, it continues to be an important tool for research, psychology, career counseling, and a range of other areas. Many basic common denominators do make it possible to understand learning styles, teach team-building tools, and provide focused counseling. It will also lead us to great discoveries about others and ourselves.

The real challenge comes not in reading this book. The true value comes in using a new understanding to apply this knowledge in real life, every day. Just as no one has ever learned to drive a car just by reading a manual, growth in understanding yourself and others becomes a continual journey of many steps. Some of it comes through staying aware of your Colors, strengths, and stresses, as well as those of others around you. A Colors seminar is frequently another powerful step. It creates the opportunity to put faces and names to each personality and allows you to *live* the lessons of this book in three dimensional and practical ways.

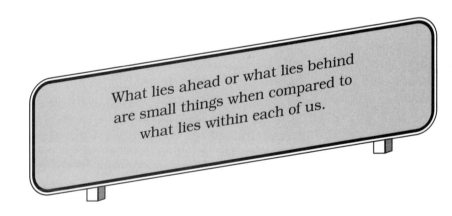

What lies ahead or what lies behind are small things when compared to what lies within each of us.

Chapter 2

The Beginning
of Personality Types

From the beginning of humankind our species has been blessed with many talents, skills, and diversities. Among them are our abilities to think, reason, learn, and grow. Along with these comes our thirst for knowledge and our drive for understanding.

In earlier times, learning revolved mainly around survival and the need to figure out how things worked. As humankind evolved and populations expanded, it became clearer that we all have different talents and unique abilities. Some of these are learned, while others appear to be inherent in our personalities. Since it has always been more logical and practical for humans to live in groups – which later became communities, towns and cities – it also increased our need to interact and get along with others. So, for literally thousands of years, humans have been studying each other. While we are certainly all unique and special, there are distinct characteristics that groups of people have in common.

The study of personality types dates back to the ancient Greeks. It was around 400 BC that a Greek by the name of Hippocrates first identified four different humors in body types. His theory was that on the physical level, these four things needed to be in balance for good health.

In modern times, the Swiss psychologist and anthropologist Carl Jung refined this study of personality types. It was Jung who first categorized individuals as being introvert or extrovert. His study of personality preferences lead Jung to see repeated behaviors that he identified into patterns. He referred to them as four psychological types. Jung believed that parents, society, and one's environment may have played a small roll in this preference, however, fundamentally individuals were already born with their natural personality types. He defined these essential functions as Sensing, Thinking, Feeling, and Intuition.

Using Jung's research as a significant resource, Katherine Briggs completed her many years of research on the same subject. Just as with Jung, it was her belief that the many, and seemingly random, behaviors in humans were in fact very orderly, identifiable, and could be described in various categories. Along with her daughter, Isabel Briggs-Myers, Katherine Briggs developed the Myers-Briggs Type Indicator™ (MBTI) which was published in 1956. The basis of her work categorized temperament characteristics into sixteen specific types. Significant validation and testing since that time has proven its validity over many years. Its success and broad application greatly increased interest in personality and temperament theory in the general population. Today, it is still widely used throughout the world.

Dr. David Keirsey, a clinical psychologist, refined the work of Myers-Briggs in 1978. Using the MBTI™ and the theories of Carl Jung, Keirsey returned to the basics of classifying personalities into four base temperaments. He published his work in the well known and widely read book *Please Understand Me*.

Another step was the development of True Colors™ in 1979. David Keirsey was a mentor to a California teacher named Don Lowry. Lowry translated the four distinct personality types into simple language that he originally developed for the school system. His goal, and his biggest achievement, was to modify complex material into everyday language. In fact, the introduction is sometimes presented as a stage production using actors to portray the four personality types.

From ancient times until today, the use of colors has been associated with everything from marketing and behavior descriptions to interior decorating. Blue is the color of the sky and the seas. In nature and decorating, it is a color that represents calm, harmony and peace and has always been thought of as a very warm color. Orange is certainly much bolder and stands out above the crowd. It is a color that is certainly very noticeable and says "look at me". It is easy to see that this color exudes energy and action.

Gold is the color of one of the most desired metals throughout history. Expressions such as "the gold standard" and others imply conservative, stability, tradition and dependability. As Green is the main color of nature, it is very much connected with thoughts of growth, abundance and creativity.

For simplicity and ease of use, describing our personality types in terms of these four Colors is certainly one of the most effective and user-friendly methods.

However, just knowing another person's particular personality type or Color accomplishes little unless it is actually used to achieve effective communication. The real challenge is to use the understanding of personality types and differences to overcome the barriers in interpersonal communication. For many, it means using the tools to understand, and not to attempt to change others to become more like themselves. As David Keirsey wrote so accurately: *"Attempts to change the spouse, offspring, student, or employee can create a change, but the result is a scar – not a transformation."*

Chapter 3

Golds

Duty and Responsibility

The confidence to plan the work and work the plan

The motto of: "Always be prepared"

A favorite sayings: "My word is my bond"

Prefers to plan and execute

A classic line:

"I know I'm right it's either black or white"

I Believe

"I believe in following through on commitments and having others know that I am dependable, prepared, and punctual. I am very loyal and understand what is right and wrong in life. I strongly value my home, family, and traditions. I am a faithful and caring friend that loves helping others and fulfilling my sense of belonging. I plan things out properly and follow orderly and concrete steps to see things through to completion."

The Sense of Duty

The core needs for Golds are founded in their strong sense of duty and responsibility. A large majority of their strengths and joys revolve around these two motivators. Many times, they accomplish this through volunteering and helping others. It ranges from continuously going the extra mile at work, to helping others through service clubs or in their community. Golds value lending a hand to others in numerous unique ways and through many acts of service. It is one of the most significant ways Golds build their self-esteem. Their motto is that hard work means success, and they take their sense of loyalty and responsibility very seriously. To Golds, their word really is their bond.

One Thing At a Time

The vast majority of Golds function best when dealing with one project at a time. They prefer to actually get it fully completed, do it very well, and then move on. It allows them to focus and to see things through to conclusion. Golds are very efficient and are great time managers that work accurately to deadlines. That does create stress when they have taken on too much, or are required to do extensive multi-tasking. It is easiest to imagine the mind of Golds similar to that of a timer. When they have taken something on, this mental timer has started. Whether the deadline is external or self-imposed, there is (preferably) only one timer in existence. Until that particular task is completed and the timer re-started as it were, they are committed and focused solely to see that matter through to completion. Golds will readily admit that a number of projects on the go at the same time, or various *gotta do* things put on their desk are a surefire way to rapidly increase their stress level.

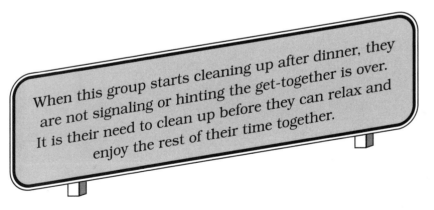

When this group starts cleaning up after dinner, they are not signaling or hinting the get-together is over. It is their need to clean up before they can relax and enjoy the rest of their time together.

It can become stressful to Golds when others are inserted into the middle of their process, or when they need to rely on others to complete sections of a project. While they are very good team players as well as cooperative and helpful, they often prefer to do specific projects from start to finish.

It allows them to be the quality control experts and to be sure that it will be done when promised, and to their satisfaction.

Making the Lists

Golds love making lists - everywhere and for every occasion. With the strong desire to get the job done, it corresponds to getting it off their list. Whether it is written, or simply in their minds, it is an ever-present reminder and motivator of what still needs to be done. Few things are as satisfying to them as crossing each and every item off their list. It is the real measure of success for a Gold. Others prefer to do their work-list before leaving at the end of the day. For them, it is the to-do list for the following day. It often gives their minds permission to relax a little, as the list, schedule and plan is ready for the following day. In either case, the danger of these lists occurs when unplanned work shows up. It may well mean that Golds realize even before lunch that the day cannot be a success when there appears little hope of getting the list completed.

I can understand how losing your to-do list is stressful. But you'll make a new one by tomorrow at the latest, I promise.

They will frequently admit that when discovering they are out of milk they generally prefer to go to the store then and there instead of adding it to the *tomorrow list*. It may not seem very efficient, but for Golds it is one more thing off their minds – a completed task has great value to them.

A large part of what makes Golds successful managers and loyal and reliable employees is their ability to focus well on the task at hand, and to be counted on to finish what they start. Therefore, getting things done and having closure is a great thrill for them. Few things satisfy Golds more than making a decision, fulfilling it, and moving on. It is definitely planning the work and working the plan.

Most often, Gold is planning the next moment, the next thing they have to do, instead of enjoying the here and now. Even at a great party, any desire to stay will almost always be overridden by the drive to get going because other things are still left to do.

Golds prefer to make a decision, stick with it, and see it through to completion. It creates stress when plans need to be changed or decisions re-visited. After all, it puts things back on the list, which is viewed as a time-waster to re-open matters that had previously been decided. In the same way, it is a real stress when their list has been misplaced. Although Golds tend to be the least likely group to misplace anything because of their strong organizational skills, being without their lists often compares to being lost without a compass.

A great strength of Golds is in the designing of plans, systems, and procedures. They derive significant comfort from fixed routines, structure, and organization. This is very much their comfort zone and where they tend to shine. This is especially true when they have had a hand in developing the systems and structures, as Golds like to participate in decision-making. In their eyes, there is great safety and satisfaction in established, tried and true, traditional routines that are not subject to daily change or fluctuation. The status-quo also applies to their life outside of work. Just the knowledge that things are on track, on time, and that the routine is working is Heaven for Golds.

Stress comes for Golds immediately after agreeing to take something on, and not at the actual deadline. Their core need and drive is to get it done. They will start a file, do an outline, plan a timetable, and start working diligently from beginning to end. Fun is for after work – right now they have a job to do, they've given their word, and others are relying on them.

Ask any Gold when they are most likely to start planning, worrying, or stressing about a project or task they are committed to. At 10 a.m. when they make the promise, or closer to 4 p.m. when it's due? Most will tell you it's at 10 a.m. when they start planning and worrying how to get it done right and on-time.

Is too much planning and organizing a strength or a stress? Here again, the opinion is influenced by someone's primary Color. For the other three groups, these traits tend to be viewed more as nuisances rather than strengths. For Golds, however, it is a large part of their comfort zone to be prepared, organized, and in control.

A Special Gold Stress

Golds describe themselves as strict rule followers. They value the safety and structure of following policies, rules, and being very law-abiding. It therefore stands to reason that following all the rules should mean that everything will turn out well. They believe that doing right leads to getting the rewards. It is a natural way for them to think and feel. It applies to relationships as well when Golds feel they are being the right kind of parent and good partner to their spouse. This is also the case at work, where they measure it through doing their job to the best of their ability, by always being on time, lending a hand where they are needed, and by having the feeling of always earning their way. When Golds follow all the rules and play their role in life *by-the-book*, it gives them a feeling of safety and security.

However, society does not judge things the same way, nor do others just fall into line with this expected outcome. Gold people still get divorced and laid-off. They still have the same quantity of crappy things happen to them as others in society. To the Golds it stands to reason that if they have played by the rules, everything will turn out well. When that is not the case, it becomes a significant stress for them. When Golds have followed all the rules, and things still don't turn out the way they're supposed to, it is a difficult reality to face.

Managing Time

Their duel talents of planning and organizing means Golds thrive by being on time. One of the biggest ways to honor them is to respect this need. A 2 p.m. meeting means 2 p.m., not 2:05. Expressed or implied, being late those five minutes sends a clear message to a Gold that you do not value them, or respect their time. In return, a Gold's promise to meet at a specific time will most certainly be fulfilled.

**Mr. Tibin is here for the meeting.
He's 3 minutes late - I assume he gets
the standard lecture first?**

A well known corporation in Vancouver, British Columbia is owned by a very high Gold. Whether legend or fact, the story of how managers meetings are conducted has been circulating for years. Apparently at the proper time these meetings are to start, the boardroom door is locked. Anyone late will simply find themselves unable to attend and terminated from the company. Only once did a manager arriving late actually take the ax from a nearby fire extinguisher box and break through the lock. His ingenuity was rewarded by him being allowed to remain in the meeting – and in his job.

Considering that same mindset, letting a Gold down by missing a deadline is akin to working with a house of cards. When someone else promises to have something done at 11 a.m., a Gold's morning is built around that time. When the task isn't completed at 11 a.m., but turns into 1 p.m., it is like taking a card out of the middle of the structure. Like the house of cards that collapses, the missed deadline will have serious ripple effects on the balance of their day. The biggest way to honor Golds is to be on time, and to deliver as promised. Their mindset demands no less, and it is not an area of their life where they will compromise very easily.

The perception that others are wasting their time is one of the highest stresses for Golds. From line-ups to broken promises, from excessive small talk to inefficiencies and changing decisions, these are the areas that drive them nuts.

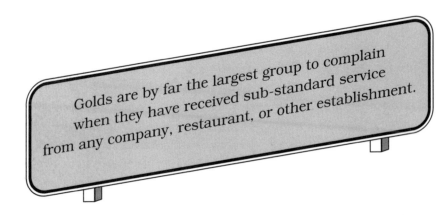

Golds are by far the largest group to complain when they have received sub-standard service from any company, restaurant, or other establishment.

A great expression for Golds is to under promise and over deliver. It is always a pleasant surprise to receive a call that an order is ready early, or that their car is fixed ahead of schedule. While they won't change their original timetable, it is one of the simple yet powerful ways for any business to retain this largest group of clients. But Golds just know this never really happens.

Like a Rock. Companies know how to market to personality types. This Bob Seger song has been used for over a decade by General Motors. Like a Rock– stable, strong, dependable, my word is my bond, you can rely on me – these are all traits which describe Golds.

Tried, Tested, and True

Ask almost any Gold to name their favorite restaurant. Then ask them to name a second favorite, if they have one. Perhaps half the Golds volunteer a second choice of restaurants. When pushed for a third, the answer most frequently is "no – it's just the first two". So the next question to ask is what they order at their favorite restaurant. Almost always they have an idea of what they generally order. This is a big learning lesson for others. Golds value stability and the comfort of having *tried-and-true* consistency. "Why would I need a third favorite restaurant? Of course I know what I'm ordering before getting there. I'm not taking a chance on something I might not like. I always order the same thing – why wouldn't I? Since it's my favorite, I know what to expect and that it'll taste great."

Those are typical Gold answers. When others are impressed that they have such a quick ability to decide what to order, that's not really the case. The Gold person has mulled over their decision before ever entering the restaurant – often looking through the menu just becomes the polite thing to do.

Linda was looking forward to dinner out with her best friend. She always enjoyed her girlfriend's Orange personality and her high energy. Linda learned long ago not to meet her friend at the restaurant since she would always be on time, but her Orange friend sometimes could be almost half an hour late. To avoid that stress, she always arranged to meet at the office instead. They had decided on the restaurant already and Linda was looking forward to ordering her favorite entrée all afternoon.

Half way to the restaurant, her Orange friend exclaims "Hey, let's go for Chinese food instead," and proceeds to head to an entirely different restaurant. Linda's mindset immediately went into shock, "We made a plan, we agreed, I've been looking forward to this – we can't change restaurants now – I've never been there – oh no – this is NOT good." The change of plans put a significant damper on Linda's enjoyment of the night. The fun and high energy she had looked forward to in being with her friend had turned into a stressful change of plans.

It is critical to honor their strong Gold values of keeping their word, sticking to their agreements, and staying on time and on track.

True to Their Word

These are the Generals of the world, and great middle managers in all kinds of businesses and industries. The Gold mentality is "tell me what to do and let me do it". When they give their word that something will be done, it will happen. It is not fun for Golds when someone feels the need to follow-up for a progress report before it is due. When they are asked "how are you making out with that report for 4 p.m.?" and it's lunch time, what the Gold mind-set hears is "I don't trust that you'll have this done on time, so I thought I'd better check up on you."

There is a big difference between what a Gold is hearing, and what the other person is actually asking. A valid reminder is that it is not always about what is being said, but more about what the other person hears. Perception and reality are often as far apart as the talking and listening.

With their strong sense of duty and responsibility, Golds believe that their word is their bond, and it is something they also expect from others. Only rare and extenuating outside circumstances could ever keep them from honoring their commitments. Any need for a progress report is very much an insult to the Gold mindset. From the big deals to the smallest details, Golds will always take care of it.

I committed to have the project done by today. Just wanted to find you and tell you I've kept my word and it's finished.

It is easy to see that Golds prefer clear and specific instructions. Few things annoy them more than when procedures apply most of the time, but then they are asked to use their discretion. "Do it this way, but then at other times go ahead and do it another way when you have to," are instructions which can make them nervous. They view things as black or white, right or wrong, and procedures that have exceptions, deviations, or options can make them very uncomfortable.

Understanding the need for stability and tradition also means becoming aware of the Gold challenges in accepting significant changes in routines, procedures, or structures. Since no person functions solely in their primary Color, during times of change their second Color influences their reactions as well. To affect changes, especially in the workplace, requires patience, communication, and time.

Golds need to buy-in to any changes, and prefer to have some options and input. They value a clear outline of the reasoning, benefits, and time-line. Pushing through significant changes without addressing these areas becomes not only a large stress to them, but can also lead to significant backlash and resistance. If a Gold's second color is Blue, for them any change also needs to address how it affects people in the process, which is discussed in a later chapter.

This is a group that places huge value on family and friends. Their idea of friends will be quite different than others, as it is generally restricted to three or four friends – but ones who have become life-long friends. There is very little Golds won't do for you if you are in this group, as they are very protective of you and will almost never refuse any request for help. Golds are very supportive and trustworthy, and possess a strong sense of dedication toward any relationship. This also includes loyalty to their employer, where image and reputation are strongly valued. Even if they win the lottery, Golds will give the proper two weeks' notice. After all, it's the right thing to do.

This is a group that wants their privacy. They set firm boundaries between work and home life. Golds place a strong value on family and friends, and a small number of life-long friendships.

Golds look for options and a bottom-line approach. This ranges from buying a product, attending a meeting or workshop and functioning at their job, to interacting in a relationship. They seek practicality and getting on with things. Since they value their organizational strengths, it means that Golds are stressed by almost anything messy or cluttered. From their desks to their manner of dress or communication style, Golds exude organization. It is certainly the Golds that invented the saying "touch a piece of paper once."

With the emphasis on short and to-the-point conversations, Golds tend to talk in list form ways, itemizing things as they speak. They also tend to want to argue in that format. They subscribe to an organized list-like method – first we'll talk about this, then that, and so on.

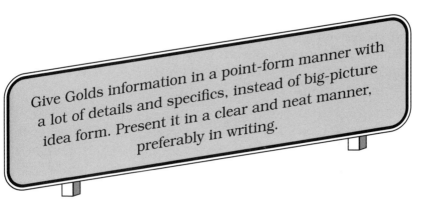

Give Golds information in a point-form manner with a lot of details and specifics, instead of big-picture idea form. Present it in a clear and neat manner, preferably in writing.

In most circumstances, they are generally not risk takers. Golds are more conservative in their dress, actions, and views. This also makes them quite practical and detail-oriented, and not a group interested in being sold on concepts. That type of approach will quickly make a Gold impatient, as they would far prefer to get a list of the tangible results or goals.

Borrowing Stuff

Golds are quite conflicted when others ask to borrow something. In fact, they hope others don't ask at all. While they have a hard time saying no, Golds are also very reluctant to lend out their possessions. They take very good care of their stuff and know that most people don't share this attitude. Plus they will become mad when something is not returned promptly, yet will have a very hard time saying anything directly. It's even worse when something like a book is finally returned and the spine is broken, or the book is marked up. In that case, it is likely most Golds will simply buy a new and undamaged copy.

Knowing that Golds have their to-do lists means anything they borrow will be returned promptly. After all, they believe it is a big responsibility to be entrusted with someone else's possessions. It will also be returned in the same condition as they received it.

Recognizing a Gold

Golds tend to wear traditional and conservative attire, and appear more formal in their demeanor. They are generally private and reserved, polite but not gushy. Remember that they value a bottom-line approach, and more often you'll hear that in their conversations.

They prefer an organized workspace, and their homes are also quite neat and tidy. They like functional and practical – definitely without clutter. Often there will be bulletin boards and lots of lists, memo pads, or sticky notes. Golds like to have clocks in plain view, or they will frequently look at their watch. Knowing what time it is can be like having a compass for the day. You'll often spot them by their day timers, Palm Pilots, or extensive organizers.

When you're listening to Golds, their voice tends to be very even and business-like. They'll word things in "either-or" ways with their view of many matters as black or white. Golds will ask for specifics and details. They are not interested in vague conversations. There will only be basic small talk, just enough to be polite before getting to the point. They'll want to know the rules, structure, and the chain of command, and will talk about one subject at a time before moving on. Therefore, they frequently ask closed-ended questions that look for a yes or no answer. After all, they want closure and to get things done, and this will clearly show in their conversational style.

Now I Understand...

Your strength is measuring success by getting it done. But not just done – done right, done now, and always when you've promised. In the same way, you do things because they need doing.

Unquestioningly, unwaveringly, and consistently.

I understand how you distinguish between a home and just a house, a job and a career, doing and doing right. Those are some of the special ways that set you apart from others in your views, attitudes, and values.

You look to be acknowledged for your efforts. So often, they are over and above what anyone could ask. "Like a Rock" really does describe you.

Planning and doing things in good order creates a sense of stability and safety in the future and for those around you.

You are a private person and don't allow everyone into your life. I feel special and honored because you are a true friend, not just a buddy.

You really can't say "No" very often. Your strong sense of duty always shows when you help others and when you give back to your community in many special ways.

No one is harder on themselves than you are - most often needlessly. When it is in moderation, it is the drive that keeps you on-task and focused.

You don't live in the past but keep many special traditions and values alive that provides an invaluable link to the future.

I am your boss or your friend. I am your partner, someone you work with or your relative and now I understand you a little better.

Common Gold Strengths

Accurate & detail-oriented	Broad shoulders
Caring & compassionate	Cautious & traditional
Clear expectations	Confident
Conscientious	Conservative
Considerate & empathetic	Consistent & dependable
Conventional & traditional	Decisive & in control
Direct & efficient	Fair, honest & compassionate
Family & friends	Focused – don't waste time
Giving & helpful	Great savers
Home is our castle	Leaders & great managers
Loyal	Organized & planning
Practical	Predictable
Punctual	Reasonable
Responsible & reliable	Right more often than wrong
Self-motivated	Self-confident
Sense of accomplishment	Solid as a rock - word is our bond
Stable & structured	Strong willed
Supportive & team players	Take blame & move on
Take charge	Thorough

Common Gold Stresses

Acting before plan in place

Always having an agenda

Automated phone systems

Being late, or anyone who is

Being put on the spot

Being taken advantage of

Change & lack of routines

Clutter & anything unorganized

Difficulty in delegating

Don't like to lose control

Emotions bottled up

Equipment that doesn't work

Exceptions to rules

Feeling overworked & frustrated

Getting sidetracked

Hard time saying no

Hard to trust others

Having everyone depend on us

Having to clean up
   other's messes

Having to wing it

Impatience

Incompetence or laziness

Inefficiency & line-ups

Interruptions

Lack of clear instructions

Last minute changes

No loyalty or lack of respect

Non-productive meetings
   and discussions

Not enough time – ever

Others deciding priorities

Others who can't make
   a decision

Paranoia over details

People that don't
   follow through

Questioning us

Reactive and scrambling

Regret taking on too much

Stuck with too much
   responsibility

Too many things undone

Unpredictability

Worrying too much

Chapter 4

Blues

Relationships and Authenticity

The confidence to put their hearts into anything they believe in

The motto of looking out for others less fortunate than themselves

A favorite saying: "Can't we all just get along?"

Want to appreciate the moment without analysis

A classic line: "Winning isn't everything – harmony is"

I Believe

"I believe that my most important goal in life is to touch others and to contribute in making this a better world for us all. I am unique and authentic. I value my relationships and reach out to others through my warmth, compassion, and caring. I'm an idealist and quite intuitive. I look for unity and harmony and love teamwork. I value caring and sharing with others in order to help them realize their dreams and unlimited potential, and I value playing a small part in helping them grow."

Relationships

Most everything in the life of Blues revolves around the main theme of relationships. Their list of strengths and joys at the end of the chapter clearly shows that life revolves around other people in almost every way. Caring for others, making the world a better place, and smoothing things over are just some of the awesome traits Blues use to describe themselves. In one way or another, those descriptions relate directly to their core need and strength of developing and fostering relationships with others in every area of their lives.

These core strengths make any Blue person a special friend. In a new school, job, or community, they quickly and easily connect with others in their warm and caring ways. Others intrinsically recognize them as people who look for meaningful relationships in any situation. One of their special talents is the innate ability to look for the good in others. It is what makes them such excellent caregivers, mediators, and peacemakers. Seldom will Blues be unwilling to open their heart to others.

With their kind and helpful nature, it also means they are often taken advantage of. Always knowing this is a possibility, Blues are frequently in conflict. Do they put their guard up and build walls around their heart to prevent getting hurt, or do they stay true to themselves, knowing they may get hurt again? This is often their internal battle. More often than not, living their life with an open heart will win out, where they choose to treat others as they wish to be treated.

Almost anything Blues do has a little piece of their heart in it. This ranges from homemade cards and special gifts to many other creative ways. Be cognizant of this and look for the clues they give you.

Living in the Heart

The life of a Blue happens in their heart. It is also a group that tends to be very spiritual. For them, life is lived through feelings over logic. Blues do well when following their very strong sense of intuition, guided by their sixth sense, and trusting what they feel is right. Information, feedback, and what they observe around them goes straight into their heart. Conversely, they speak in terms of feelings, rarely filtering their emotions through logic. After all, you cannot tell your heart what to do. It is what society terms "wearing your heart on your sleeve." This expression accurately describes their demeanor, and is at the core of what makes them such caring people. It is also the reason others seek out Blues for their ability to easily relate to others in meaningful and real ways. The times in life when Blues have gone off track are very directly related to not following their intuition. This group will always do well following their heart. It also means they are able to spot a phony a mile away. Sales staff and many others have no chance with Blues without first connecting with them through a genuine relationship and actually caring about them.

I know you're concerned and nervous, but when I said we should talk, I just meant about my dreams and feelings and stuff...

When life revolves around feelings, there is also a downside. It has Blues deeply affected by criticism, harsh words, or cruelty. Their strong motivation for peace and harmony makes them very sensitive to conflict or injustice. These inequities go against everything they believe in and fight for, and create significant stress in their life. Hence, they can often view criticism as a personal attack, leading to misinterpretation of comments received from others, no matter how carefully worded. Whether true or not, their natural reaction is to get their feelings hurt.

Giving in to the Needs of Others

Blues will readily admit there are times when they feel taken advantage of. At best, they certainly have a great tendency to bend to the wishes of others, or the will of any group. Learning the lesson of asking for something for themselves, or standing up for what they want, is a difficult challenge. What comes naturally is sacrificing their own wishes and desires in order to accommodate others, and to fit in and feel needed, included, and part of the team.

"Delaying your own life is a waste, if you are waiting for the aproval of others, while robbing yourself of many things that matter to you. Don't confuse it's not important with I'm not important – because others may."

It is very common for Blues not to make waves, and they rarely come across as selfish. This often makes it a challenge to see when they are hurting, or having a difficult time, before it builds up into an emotional outburst.

Blues are very active listeners who love communicating and connecting with people in real and meaningful ways. They ask open-ended questions and love an answer longer than one word. It also means when they supply one word answers, it may be time to dig further, as there may be a problem.

Communication Skills

Blues are very good communicators, by any measure. When they ask someone "How are you?" they really do want to know. When they wish someone a great day, they really do mean it. Blues are also very good listeners. It is one of their great strengths, making other Colors quickly realize that this is the group to seek out when they need a shoulder to cry on, or someone to just listen to them without fixing or judging.

Desiring deep and meaningful conversations can also get their feelings easily hurt when others are abrupt, phony, or short. There are many times when others walk past Blues without acknowledging their greetings. Often it is a Gold or Green, deep in thought, or in the middle of a task. While it may seem trivial, it has a measurable effect on Blues. Their immediate reaction is to wonder what they did wrong, or why that person is mad at them. To others, that example is clearly not about the Blue person at all, as they have quite a different outlook on a seemingly inconsequential communication.

Blues value open communication where feelings are shared and everyone is included. They enjoy small talk, which builds meaningful relationships. To them, really getting to know someone means taking the time to communicate and actively listening. Only then can Blues utilize their sense of intuition in understanding and connecting with others.

Our Blue friends are very positive and optimistic. They look for possibilities and the good in everything, strongly valuing discussions of their dreams and ideas in safe situations where they will not be laughed at, judged, or compared to others.

Because of their inability to be selfish, they will also tend to talk around the point, or sugarcoat conversations. By understanding this, it is important to communicate with them in direct and specific ways to keep conversations on track. The lesson for Blues is in understanding that communication requires clarity, and clarity requires a backbone to tell it like it is – something that is not easily accomplished for them.

"You heard me, you loved me, you gave me a gift.
My spirit was broken but you gave it a lift.
You trust me, you know me, you mention my name.
To reach out to others who might feel the same.
I feel safe and secure and never ashamed.
Alone I feel guilty, alone I feel blamed.
But when we're together and we really do share,
my burdens are lifted, because you really do care."
S. Smith

Blues strongly value frequent positive verbal affirmations and recognition for their uniqueness and contributions to others and their team.

The Value of a Hug

In a perfect world, Blues would much rather receive a genuine hug than a handshake. After all, their prime motivation is to connect with people from the heart. In relationships, they value both quality and quantity time together. In the excellent book "*The Five Love Languages*," author Gary Chapman describes five distinct *languages* everyone speaks in showing or receiving affection. Two of these are physical touch and spending quality time together. While there may not be a direct connection to each group's Colors, both of these are quite important to almost all Blues. Holding hands, cuddling on the couch, arms around their partner – these and many other methods are natural ways Blues validate their feelings of being cared for and needed.

In this same manner, Blues also share their affection with others. They are easily recognized as connecting with people through a soft touch on the shoulder, a warm handshake, or a caring hug that comes from the heart. How sad that one of the greatest joys for Blues has become somewhat unacceptable, or perhaps politically incorrect, in today's society.

Don't get your feelings hurt. This is a positive. I'm going to teach you to stand up for yourself and learn to say no, Thompson!

Ask for What You Want

It is a very real challenge for Blues to ask for anything for themselves. Their overriding desire to care for others makes the Blue person feel that standing up for their needs is a sign of selfishness. Hence, they will seldom express their own needs. This creates the special challenge for others to stay aware of the Blues' needs and feelings. Learning to "take care of yourself so you can take care of others" is a powerful and valuable lesson for Blues, but so hard to learn.

Blues will spend their entire day helping those around them, listening to their needs, and truly feeling the pain of others. Seldom will they say no to anyone, or refuse to lend a hand. This results in a very real difficulty in setting boundaries. They will constantly attempt to smooth things over, and will always ensure that everyone feels included. It is a group that relates very well to the underdog and can easily substitute their own plans or wishes with those of other people, just to get along. At the end of the day, they can frequently admit to being quite run-down and exhausted. Even with no real desire for alone time, these become occasions when Blues just need to re-charge their batteries and get away from everyone. If one of the big questions in life is whether someone is a giver or a taker, it is an easy answer when judging the Blue person.

"The key in life is in finding balance.
That fine line between helping those less fortunate than you
while taking care of yourself first. Sometimes that starts by
practicing to say no without feeling guilty. Starting with
minor things and slowly working up to bigger ones."

It's Never Enough

A big stress for Blues is their continuous feeling that they could have, or should have, done more. Helping others is a great way for Blues to build their self-esteem. It comes very natural for them, and it never crosses their mind to first consider what's in it for them. The side effect of this is that Blues seldom believe that they have done enough, whether measured by what else they could have done, or who else they could have reached out to. It is a never-ending cycle for them, frequently concentrating on what else they could have done, and not focusing on the positive impact they actually did have. With their easy-going nature and never-ending efforts to care for others, Blues often become the unsung heroes who can frequently be taken for granted.

Blues have a very strong motivation for peace at all cost. Consequently, they will be the great peace-makers and seek to include everyone. It also means that they will give into many things to maintain this peace even when it goes against their wishes or desires, always bending to the will of others.

One of the best known Blue personalities in the world, along with Princess Diana, was certainly Mother Theresa. In a 1958 letter, she wrote: "My smile is a great cloak that hides a multitude of pains." Without a doubt, this was one of the most loving and caring Blue people of the last century. How was it possible that this role model admired throughout the world, who lived her purpose so clearly, even considered those thoughts? It is widely believed that they could be explained for two reasons – one, in large part, was due to the overwhelming immensity of the tasks she faced, and the second reason was due to her core need to feel her love for God returned.

Making a Difference

Touching people's lives, and having a positive impact on others, is a huge reward and an incredible self-esteem builder for Blues. Their self-esteem is built in powerful ways when they can put their whole heart into something and make a difference. Nowhere does that show more clearly than the best known Blue personality alive today, Oprah Winfrey. In a world of mass media and the incredible power of television, Winfrey stands head and shoulders above others in her ability to connect with people through her heart in real and meaningful ways. When Oprah shows tears and emotions, they are absolutely genuine, as this Blue role model, or any Blue, cannot be phony or insincere.

Oprah, like almost all other Blues, combine their strong sense of optimism with dreams of making a real difference in the lives of others. For her, it was the dream of reaching a million children orphaned in Africa, which started in late 2003. While that number may have seemed unrealistic to many, in one way or another she will surely touch many more with her dream and purpose to put the faces of real children with the impersonal numbers reported by the media.

While it is pure speculation, at times even such a powerful role model may sometimes question whether she was really making a difference and touching lives. Blues value seeing the impact they make on others in direct ways, which is quite different from hoping or seeing it through television, books, or other indirect ways. This is certainly evident when Oprah shared that her Africa trip rated amongst the most memorable moments in her life.

Amidst rumors of her retirement in the fall of 1998, Oprah re-focused the show to reflect a new theme of "change your life television." Now even the theme of the show reflected her strong drive to have an impact on people. Born at the beginning of an era of hope, she truly does touch millions in deep and meaningful ways even Oprah may not always realize, or acknowledge. In the words of her best friend, Gayle King on A&E's Biography, "She gets a tremendous high when she knows she's helped someone." There is truly no better way to describe a life lived with purpose and meaning every day, in so many ways, for Oprah, or any Blue.

Inclusion

Blues have a strong need to feel included. Few things are as hurtful to them as being excluded from a group function or activity. A primary fear for all of us is the fear of rejection. It is, however, much stronger for Blues than for others. When life is lived through feelings, they become very sensitive in this area. A group of coworkers going for lunch without them, or finding out friends had a get-together and didn't invite them, can leave Blues feeling hurt and rejected. It is a hurt that will last longer than with others. To compound matters, since Blues are very unselfish, they will often never say anything.

Excluded and rejected is often how the heart of a Blue perceives this. Whether true or not, in life perception is sometimes viewed as reality. To have many Blue friends and family members is special, indeed. It does come with the "care instructions" of being sensitive to these types of situations. On the other hand, it is also valid to explain to Blues, in a caring way, that they need to tell others when their feelings are hurt. Perhaps this is an important lesson for everyone.

"There is a special person in your life that has always
been with you through all your hurts and your pains.
Someone that believes in you more than anyone else.
A best friend that has never let you down. Someone that
you can always rely on and is relentlessly cheering for
you as you grow stronger each and every day without
growing harder. That special friend is you.
Learning to trust and open your heart again always
starts from within. There is a big difference between
knowing that in your mind and feeling it in your heart

> *isn't there? A big difference between thinking it and*
> *feeling it that others do not understand.*
> *I know you'll do it - you're worth it!"*

Denise is a Blue manager in a large corporation. Without telling anyone, her Gold boss had planned the last staff conference as a two-part meeting. At the conclusion of the first portion, her boss simply asked Denise and another staff member to leave the room so they could discuss other matters. Only a Blue person could understand how hurtful that was. Without explanation, and in a matter-of-fact way, she was being excluded from the group. Her first reaction was to use humor to deflect from her true feelings that were about to come to the surface. Once outside the boardroom, this quickly became anger and frustration, followed by a good cry. When

Blues will forgive but almost never forget. It is important to be sensitive to their feelings, as they will not supply you feedback in direct ways when they have been hurt. They may shut down, become quiet or resentful, but will not often verbalize their hurt feelings.

another staff member came in, others started to see through Denise's eyes the manner in which she and her coworker were dismissed from the meeting. As it turned out, less than half the group even noticed what happened. When two staff members who understood a little about Denise's personality offered her a hug, she actually refused. The great Blue sense of intuition and ability to spot a phony clearly saw that this was more patronizing than real.

Part of the Team

A tremendous Blue strength involves being excellent team players. With their desire for relationships and harmony, working as a group is a natural gift for them. That also makes them great team builders with their sensitivity to the needs of others. They are strong believers in fostering an environment of inclusion, and they always seek to create motivational environments. To work independently of others can quickly drain them of their energy source of being part of the team.

The Blue heart seeks this constant interaction with others and a sense of belonging. They truly love feeling they are needed by others. Their desire for teamwork manifests itself in the strong ability to share work, responsibility, and certainly the credit. They do not look to be the star nor the center of attention, and recognition is readily shared amongst their team. By clearly putting others before the tasks at hand, Blues do admit that staying task-oriented in routines or making paperwork a priority can be a real challenge.

Recognizing a Blue

Their demeanor is always open and caring, warm and friendly. Blues enjoy touching and connecting with others in meaningful ways. They'll have pictures of family and pets around. Our Blue friends love pets, almost without exception – pets love unconditionally, which Blues know they cannot always get from people. They tend to have very animated facial expressions, and it's easy to see they're active listeners.

When listening to a Blue, you will hear that they will mainly communicate in terms of feelings instead of thoughts. They use humor and laughter in conversation and ask many open-ended questions designed to encourage others to express themselves with more than yes or no answers. They really want to get to know people, and express lots of empathy and caring in their tone and speech. Everyone quickly notices their soothing voice and calm, welcoming tone. They will also seek to smooth many things over and say "I'm sorry" a lot – even when it's not their fault.

Now I Understand...

You give and give and can frequently run on empty. I need to learn to be sensitive to your needs before you ask and be aware that you have a hard time saying no. You are a loyal friend, a great partner, someone I love spending time with. You keep dreams and possibilities alive and always look for the good and the positive in everyone and everything.

I understand that when you talk I don't need to fix. I just need to listen in the same caring way that you always do. Not judging, not fixing, and not being critical – just listening. Because you open your heart so often, so easily, I need to always be mindful to step gingerly.

I want to help you choose ways to take care of yourself. After all, it is only when you take care of yourself that you can take care of others.

Almost everything you do has a little piece of your heart in it. A little part of you is in every project and conversation, and in many other areas of your life. You value putting your heart into everything you truly believe in.

You have a great sense of intuition. You listen to it and follow it and you are right more often than not. It also means I don't have to put on an act, I can always be myself, because you will not reject the real me.

I marvel at your ability to connect with others so easily in spiritual and meaningful ways. You don't just define the word friendship, you live it through your words and actions every day, all day.

Finally, I will remember that your hug or a warm touch cures many things and touches others in special, caring ways.

I am your boss or your friend. I am your partner, someone you work with or your relative, and now I understand you a little better.

Common Strengths

Bringing joy to others	Caring for others
Comfortable	Compassionate
Creative	Democratic
Devoted	Easy going
Everyone has potential	Flexible
Forgiving	Friendly
Generous	Good listeners
Great huggers	Honest
Include everyone	Intuitive
Joy of living	Kind hearted
Like to laugh…and cry	Look people in the eyes
Loving and romantic	Loyal
Making the world a better place	Other people seek us out to talk
Patient	Peace-makers
Polite	Positive & eternal optimists
Quiet	Sense of humor
Sensitive	Sincere
Smooth things over	Spiritual
Sympathetic	Tactful
Totally people-oriented	Trustworthy
Warm	Won't let others down

Common Stresses

Afraid to confront others	Arguments or conflict
Being taken advantage of	Cannot please everyone
Can't say no & burnout	Cold people
Criticism & harsh tone of voice	Deadlines
Domineering people	Feeling you've never done enough
Feelings hurt easily	Frustrated by inflexibility
Intuition can cause problems	Knowing we'll get hurt again
Lack of empathy or hugs	Lack of warmth or humor
Lingering conflict & disharmony	Loud conversations
Missing romance	No communication or connection
No eye contact	Not being taken seriously when emotional
Not making time for ourselves	Paperwork
People without integrity	Phony people & pushy salesmen
Reviews – giving and getting	Square pegs-round holes
Too many others need us	Trying to be helpful
Unable to save the whole world	Unappreciated
Work before people	Worrying about others' problems

Chapter 5

Oranges

Freedom and Skillfulness

The confidence to wing it and see what happens.
The motto of "Just Do It" and "Let's Go!"
Favorite sayings: "Whatever" and "Get over it"
Prefers to enjoy the spontaneity of the moment
A classic line:
"Winning isn't everything—it's the only thing!"

I Believe

"I believe that life is a game to be played to win with fun, variety, creativity, and not too much planning or structure. I love competition and interacting with other people. I avoid boredom and routines at almost all cost. I'm a natural troubleshooter who doesn't mind rolling up my sleeves and getting involved hands-on. I greatly value my skills, freedom, courage, and high energy level. I'm ready and able to act on a moment's notice – just watch me!"

It is always easy to spot a high Orange as they enjoy being noticed and recognized. They stand out, and don't mind at all attracting attention to themselves. They believe in being unique, which is achieved through the latest, greatest, and coolest stuff. From the clothes they wear to the cars they drive, image is very important, and they act, talk, and dress like winners. Almost anything that says "notice me" greatly appeals to them. In many ways, Oranges love to be trendsetters and stand out above the crowd.

Talking with Oranges

Communication styles are quite different for Oranges, which is often a real challenge for the rest of the world. Communicating with them is best done in person or on the telephone. Oranges love interaction, back-and-forth exchanges, and immediate reactions. This immediacy is what creates their need for interactive conversations, which cannot be accomplished by mail, fax, or e-mail. That is certainly one of the reasons Oranges have such challenges in school and in most companies, which are institutions structured and administered by Gold people.

Keep it short, positive, and make it quick! Oranges are not interested in explanations, questions, or information with too much theory, or irrelevant details. In general, if it can be explained in the length of time it takes for an elevator ride, it will appeal to their desire to get on with it.

Nothing is Set in Stone

To the Orange mind-set almost everything can be negotiated. Their love of competition and winning makes them powerful and successful sales people. A no to an Orange is almost always taken as a maybe instead. It often just increases the challenge for any Orange sales person. It becomes more of a chance to use their talents of charm,

**That was a gift from work, since I'm
the Queen of handling challenges
and putting out fires.**

humor, and ability to think on their feet. Assuming they even hear the word no – it's full speed ahead to pursue the sale. All that's needed is to find another angle to accomplish their goal, get their way or make the deal.

The attitude of winning, along with a drive to never fail, makes a powerful combination. When that is combined with a commission plan, recognition, or a dare, they are well on their way to being seriously motivated. Oranges have a natural gift of selling themselves, changing tracks at the drop of a hat, and speaking very fast. Their tone is highly animated with a frequent single-minded determination to get their way.

Let's Talk About Money

Money is often mentioned as both a strength and a stress for Oranges – there is just never enough of it. While that's probably also the case for everyone else, it is a different issue for this group. They will tend to make a lot of money, but they will also quickly spend it. It is rare for Oranges to first ask how much something costs. Their motto is to rationalize that if it's worth having, just buy it, as this group very much acts on impulse. In most situations it is a matter of seeing, liking, buying. In that same manner, they are also very generous with their friends, family, and others when it comes to money.

> This group filters most information against the scale of "What's in it for me? Is it practical? Bottom line—can I use this today?" This includes sales presentations, meetings, purchases, feedback, seminars, and all other areas of their life.

To Oranges, just having to track expenses is a hassle seldom worth worrying about. "If I want something, I'm buying it" is their attitude. It is no wonder that large numbers of them are motivated by commissions and bonus plans. It allows Oranges to directly do whatever it takes to control the size of their paycheck. For them, it is a concrete motivation which allows them to live the lifestyle they choose, and to be rewarded in direct proportion to their talents and efforts.

Oranges will readily rise to any challenge and will accept almost any dare. This is often as easy as pointing out that something can't be done or that nobody has ever managed to do it before. Just hearing this type of comment gets their attention and provides them the opportunity to be the star. This is especially true when there are tangible rewards and recognitions involved.

Releasing Some Energy

The two most common New Year's resolutions are to work out and to get organized. The former does not frequently apply to Oranges. Most have realized long ago, that being physically active acts as an important outlet for their pent-up energy. They are some of the most faithful members of fitness or running clubs as they love almost anything physical. It can be walking, mountain biking, swimming, or any form of team sports. After a week of having no physical exercise, they tend to become more fidgety and a little stir-crazy. Many Oranges that do not work out still have their built-in exercise through being constantly on their feet and always on the go during the day. For anyone who has ever attended a long conference with Oranges, they will be the ones taking advantage of any breaks to walk around the block, or to do something physical. They know full well that sitting through an entire presentation is a real challenge that requires them to release some energy before they are able to sit again for any length of time.

The resolution of getting organized is a challenge of a different kind. Chances are that resolution will be on the list again for the foreseeable future.

Oranges in Sports

A large number of professional sport personalities are high Orange. It is not because of the large pay, although that certainly becomes one of the benefits. Every day is different, there is continuous competition, and others share their attitude that winning is everything. Competition and winning are always high on the Orange agenda. It is the great rush of adrenaline and constant challenges that motivates Oranges.

Yup, I'll try anything once. I live life on the edge all right! Edge, ledge...whatever...

Yes, even sports have rules to follow. But overall this environment involves the survival of the fittest, not too much structure, and unique situations requiring constant adaptation, change, and creativity that greatly appeals to Oranges.

At work or in relationships, Oranges will start looking for another position, or consider breaking up if things to become too restricted, with too many rules, or when the fun is gone, whether real or perceived.

A Special Orange Challenge

A number of studies in the criminal justice system show that Oranges comprises a disproportionate percentage of penitentiary inmates. Does that make Oranges just *bad actors*? Not at all. The rules, created by a Gold society, do not fit the Oranges' style or personality. Oranges typically challenge boundaries and the status quo in many situations. They do have a strong value system, but it is all their own. Some were either never taught, or aren't interested, in learning what others consider appropriate behavior.

On the other side of the coin is the huge group of extremely successful Oranges. Large numbers of them are self-employed, and highly successful entrepreneurs, managers, and CEOs. The Oranges who conform within the basic rules and norms that society has set have not lost their uniqueness at all. When their energies and personality traits are channeled in positive directions they become almost unstoppable.

Hurry Up

Our Orange friends love speed, action, and everything fast. From cars to motorcycles, from conversations to hobbies and sports. Their strong need for movement, freedom, and action makes it very difficult for others to keep up. They have a never-ending drive for adventure, excitement, and keeping things moving. They are almost always upbeat and optimistic.

Around 75 percent of the population are extroverts, and it is certainly easy to see that the large majority of Oranges are in this group. They are great multi-taskers, who do anything possible to avoid boredom. Even decisions come quickly to the Orange mind. They simply don't have the time to linger over many questions and are able to make rapid decisions. At the same time, they also possess the ability to stay flexible and change tracks or plans when the situation requires it. Conversations with them often tend to jump from subject to subject, quickly covering many topics.

When they are in action their expectation is for others to keep up. Even in simple things, others need to stay sharp and on their toes. When Oranges call to make plans, it is generally just before jumping into action. Seldom will anyone have much notice to decide whether they wish to come along. If it takes too long to decide, no problem – they're going without you.

Few things are more hilarious than to see sales staff totally unable to speed up, or to switch gears, and target sales presentations to high Orange customers. The bottom line still is that they will frequently just walk out if it appears, in their judgment, that it will take too long or involve too much paperwork or hassle.

Orange detests and avoids anything slow! From traffic line-ups, from answers to decisions. They will quickly show their impatience and will avoid line-ups by simply walking out.

Winging It

As great multi-taskers, Oranges always have many things on the go at once. Frequently that means something gets dropped or they're hurrying to complete something. To help with that, Oranges have long appreciated their Gold friends and coworkers. Deadlines are a real stress to this group, but not the deadlines sometime in the future – they'll worry about it then. It is the *right now* deadlines that cause them to scramble.

They can easily be sitting at lunch and all of a sudden realizing they have a meeting to be ready for in half an hour. Don't worry – be happy – and certainly no need to panic. Too much preparation is of no interest to them. Besides, it's probably not needed. Ulcers are something Oranges might give, but they are the last group to suffer from themselves.

Oranges would far prefer to wing it, play it by ear, and see what happens. Thinking on their feet and working on anything without being fully prepared is how they function best. It means they haven't had to spend too much time preparing and it gives them the chance to amend things as they go along. As great negotiators, they certainly have the skills to pull this off. They are practical problem solvers and natural risk takers that readily accept any challenge. When it comes to written reports however, that is seldom something they enjoy.

Do not misunderstand or judge one of their greatest strengths of winging it in almost all situations. It allows them to stay reasonably stress-free, have lots on the go and remain flexible.

As a result, from their early years of school right through to the workforce, paperwork is something to be avoided at almost all cost. Many of these traits are those almost everyone had when they were younger. It is only the Orange group that is fortunate enough to retain them as they get older. Don't plan too much, think on your feet, less worry and more fun are all traits Oranges will always cherish and defend all their lives.

I know it seems horrible, but those are just office memos and policies. You only have to read them - you're not actually allergic to paperwork.

Oranges are very artistic and creative. It is a large part of what makes them very flexible and receptive to new ideas. Learning happens by hands-on doing, and not through textbooks, manuals, or policy binders. It is done through trial and error, while always pushing the envelope and experimenting as much as possible. They would rather do it than talk about it. Oranges prefer to take their ideas or plans – not fully developed – and run them by the world. The feedback, or input, either allows them to further amend their ideas, or they can decide whether they want to carry on with the plan at all. They possess a self-assured and confident attitude while remaining calm in any crisis. Changing tracks when necessary is not a problem if new or better information comes along.

ADD?

Attention Deficit Disorder (ADD) is likely something many high Oranges have been asked about, or labeled as, at one time or another. In fact, drug makers claim that over eight million adults suffer from ADD in North America. While many may, the symptoms of ADD can also easily be misinterpreted as normal Orange stresses and behaviors. The web-site of one drug maker even claims that a simple six-question test will establish whether someone is likely to have the symptoms of ADD. The questions range from whether the person has trouble finishing the details of projects, difficulty sitting still for long periods without fidgeting, or has challenges with getting started on detailed projects.

Whether those are valid questions to measure the symptoms of ADD is something only medical experts can judge. However, perhaps these broad questions simply define some high Orange stresses, which can easily be labeled, but do come with an equally impressive list of positives. These include a no-fear attitude, unshakable belief that anything is possible, awesome creativity, and drive to be constantly challenged and multi-tasking. Yes, most Orange do come with some impulsiveness, distraction, and desire to avoid paperwork as much as possible. But in the words of JetBlue Airways CEO David Neeleman during a 60 Minutes feature on adult ADD: "Your brain just thinks a little different and you come up with things. I just have a feeling that if I took the medication, I'd be just like everybody else." Critics are even harsher calling these "lifestyle drugs" in the two billion dollar ADD industry.

Friends and Buddies

Oranges have a very high energy level. They love life, have a great sense of humor, and love to laugh, always remaining the eternal optimists. They love the company of others and are very approachable and easy to talk to. It must have been an Orange that first said "don't take yourself too seriously." This makes them a magnet in attracting others. Their easy-going and fun attitude, along with a very social nature, makes them great friends for everyone. Because of these strong traits they have a large circle of friends. It is also their group to network with, something that is a particular strength for Oranges. They are always up for any night out, or a party. They won't arrive on time, but they'll be the last ones to leave, and a big factor in the energy of the party. If it's an occasion to have fun and let loose, chances are Oranges will most certainly be there, and at the front of the line.

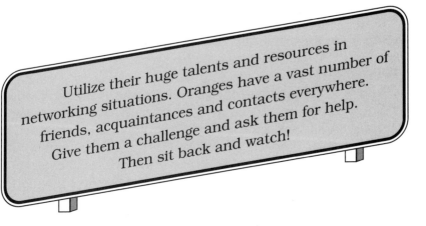

Utilize their huge talents and resources in networking situations. Oranges have a vast number of friends, acquaintances and contacts everywhere. Give them a challenge and ask them for help. Then sit back and watch!

Driving Orange Crazy

Many things do frustrate or cause stress to Oranges. To start, anything slow is of little interest to them. That covers a range of areas from meetings to other people. Anything dull or boring also fits into this category. Their desire to wing it, and to negotiate many issues, frequently makes following the rules a special challenge. With having many things on the go, Oranges can also forget things or lose them. It is always a big stress when they are stuck and delayed having to find something.

As mentioned already, Oranges in general are not particularly concerned with being organized, unless their job specifically has taught them, or requires it. Often stores advertise with the line of: "Getting organized is easy at... (insert your favorite hardware or office supply store here)." It is an advertisement everyone has seen hundreds of times over the course of a year. Unless they're sending a Gold staff member along at no charge, it is not that easy for Oranges. But then the definition of organized is in the eye of the beholder. For this group it means "don't touch my desk – I know exactly where everything is!"

Others, especially Golds, frequently judge this group by their special challenge of staying on time. Oranges often have their watches or clocks set ahead for just that reason. As they are great at juggling many tasks, and value their interactions with others, they can often be late. It is not a particular concern to them, however they do hear enough feedback from friends and bosses to make it an irritant.

Orange at Work

A special hassle is always reserved for red tape, rules, regulations, and fixed structures. Unfortunately that is the environment of most companies. Oranges tend to view these more in terms of guidelines rather than actual rules. Following fixed procedures and being stuck with routine tasks becomes a huge challenge for them. Even when Oranges enjoy their job, the largely Gold workplace means they often look forward to one minute after work ends, where real living can begin.

When looking at statistics of Oranges in the workforce, it is easy to see that they vote with their feet. The percentage entering the workforce, as compared to upper management, is very small. Where did they all go? Many chose long ago to become self-employed in an effort to avoid too much boredom, rules and restrictions. It allows them to pursue their natural curiosity to explore, test, and figure things out on their own terms. Besides, their ability to handle large amounts of risk and stress makes them perfect entrepreneurs. Working for themselves lets them have the chance to call the shots, set their own rules, and leave enough time to have fun and play.

Oranges love change and variety. When they don't have this with the company they work for, they will spend their energy in creating it instead of focusing on their job and tasks. That necessitates having the Orange employees buying into the structure of the firm, as well as the reasons and logic behind specific regulations. If that is not the case, they will often shortcut them and do things their own way. Another often used alternative to retain excellent Orange staff members is to allow them the freedom to help create and shape their own role and function within the company.

A final point worth noting is something called an *Orange moment*. These are the times when they really wish they could get the words back into their mouth. Oranges prefer to tell it like it is, although sometimes the direct *shoot from the hip* comments are difficult for others to handle. Talking or acting before thinking is often something that gets Oranges in trouble with others. But then their view is "don't ask me a question if you don't want to hear the answer!"

Oh no! Are you trying to make the Orange staff read the policy manuals again?

Recognizing an Orange

It is not difficult to spot a high Orange. They like to dress trendy and love the latest fashions. Their workspace will often be quite messy. You might also notice they tend to misplace things. Oranges have an active and very confident demeanor and you can just feel that they have lots on the go. A real challenge for them is sitting still for extended time periods, and they will exhibit lots of fidgeting, quick movements and gestures. If they have pictures up, they love including some of themselves with famous personalities.

When you listen to an Orange, you can sense that same high energy level. They love laughter and humor, and will quickly jump from subject to subject, talking quite fast or getting sidetracked. They're natural name-droppers and have a very animated tone of voice. Oranges love to network, so they'll often promote ideas or businesses and ask probing questions. They want to talk about big picture stuff instead of too many specifics or details. Keep conversations short and to the point. If an Orange wants more information, they will certainly ask.

Now I Understand...

I recognize that being on time is often a challenge and may be more important to me than to you.

The clock shouldn't measure the value of our relationships, anyway.

I value and look for your high energy that makes you a magnet to others who seek you out. I can't duplicate it, but I also gain energy from being around you.

Sometimes my role is just to finish up something or pick up the pieces. Yes, I may grumble or complain, but I also know if it weren't for you, we probably wouldn't have gotten started at all.

You teach me not to be too serious about many situations. I continue to learn that it's ok to laugh at myself. You pull me out of my shell, sometimes fighting or resisting – but don't give up.

You teach in ways others don't. Not through textbooks or talking about it. You do it by example, by rolling up your sleeves and actually doing it.

Your ability to change tracks and your "let's go" attitude is something I value learning from you.

Sometimes I may not participate, but just love watching you in action. With you there is seldom a dull moment.

Few others have your combination of talent and personality. You value freedom as much as others value knowing you. I was a lot more like you as a kid. Watching you, I sometimes wonder how the world has closed in on me, where you have managed to keep so much of your free spirit.

I am your boss or your friend. I am your partner, someone you work with or your relative and now I understand you a little better.

Common Strengths

Active	Adventurous
Artistic	Awesome sales people
Creative	Don't take things too seriously
Don't worry-be happy	Dynamic
Energizer bunnies	Entertaining & fun
Fast paced	Flexible
Freedom	Generous
Great sense of humor	Great with tools
Having fun	Impatient
Impulsive	Just do it!
Life is never boring	Love attention
Low stress	Loyal & caring
Open-minded	Optimistic
Outrageous & vocal	People magnet
Ready & able to change	Risk-takers
Skillful	Social
Spontaneous	Tell it like it is
Unpredictable	Winning

Common Stresses

Accountants, bankers, lawyers

Boredom and lack of action

Challenge to finish stuff

Fixed rules and policies

Having to be on time

Lack of choices

Making lists

Meetings & deadlines

Non-party people

Not enough recognition

Paperwork

Photo radar and speed traps

Rigid schedules

Sappy songs

Slow people

Spending time alone

Stuck inside

Uptight people

Being on the sidelines

Chained to a desk

Conformity

Hate to lose

How-to manuals

Losing things

Manuals & procedures

Needy people

Not enough challenges

Not enough money

People who ask too many questions

Political correctness

Routines

Sitting still

Sore losers

Structure & rules

Studying

Whiners, complainers & worriers

Chapter 6

Greens

Knowledge and Understanding

The confidence to know they are right, and can substantiate it with facts.

The motto of gathering the facts and options before making a decision

A favorite saying: "You want it when?"

Want to examine all experiences so they can be improved next time

I Believe

"I believe in remaining calm, cool, and collected in any situation. I value knowledge and learning and enjoy passing that knowledge onto others. I am intelligent and logical and can be a perfectionist. I am analytical and enjoy thinking things through. I want to explore all possibilities and avenues in my creative and inventive ways before committing myself or making a decision. I prefer to look at the big picture and can consistently be counted on to provide logical information and answers."

The Green mindset greatly values knowledge and understanding. They love to be constantly challenged mentally by anything or anyone. Their primary focus is to be proactive, not scrambling or reactive. They are leaders and not followers, with a sharp mind and never-ending desire to grow and learn. They are constantly thinking about, evaluating, and formulating ideas in their minds. Consequently, they are often a number of steps ahead of others in plans, ideas, and visions.

Getting caught up in routines holds little interest to Greens. These are the trend-setters and not "yes" people or followers. What others do, or conforming to the norm, is of little interest to them. Greens create and look for logic and competence, not only in processes, but also in others they work with, and in the framework or structure of their environment.

Our Green friends are very receptive to anything new and innovative. This group consists of trendsetters and visionaries, and they were certainly the primary people behind most technological advances over the past decades. However, it does not mean they will jump on something immediately without thinking it through first. They always look at all consequences, possibilities, and implications, as well as weigh the long-range effects of these changes before they commit themselves.

I've been teaching him that knowledge is power, so he's been bringing me the computer.

Information is Power

That is, indeed, a phrase that Greens strongly value. Greens tend to be very much above-average intellectually. From their childhood to retirement, Greens love to learn. This is never restricted to anything just in their field. They are almost like a sponge when it comes to both seeking and absorbing information. To them, it is a constant search for understanding the "why" and "how" questions related to almost any subject. As the Green mind is constantly processing and analyzing everything they encounter, information truly is power.

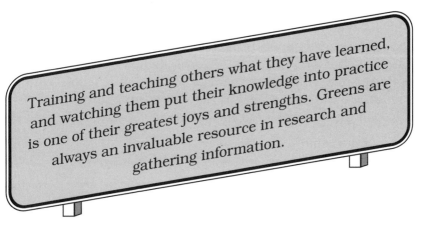

Training and teaching others what they have learned, and watching them put their knowledge into practice is one of their greatest joys and strengths. Greens are always an invaluable resource in research and gathering information.

Wondering how something works, why procedures are in place, or challenging methods that are outdated are particular Green strengths. They focus on big picture questions and implications involving complex problems. When that is accomplished, Greens are very happy with existing practices that are tested and perfected. Since they were established with the best information available, Greens accept them once they understand the "how" and "why" in a logical fashion.

The occasions when they become frustrated happen when those same procedures or methods are no longer valid or logical. When they appear to be redundant or obviously inferior in their minds, it becomes a source of contention. This is the point when their generally easy-going personality starts to resist. Greens cannot conceive how anyone can operate with sub-par procedures or operating methods when they see improvements so clearly.

That same mindset applies to attending meetings where they see decisions made without giving proper thought to implications or taking the time to make informed decisions. This preference applies to all areas of their life, where Greens value having access to basic information well in advance. It allows them time to research and analyze the material being covered. Having this time means they can be well prepared to ask relevant questions and contribute in meaningful ways. Feedback or ideas will not be forthcoming until they are able to back up their ideas or research with factual data.

Greens are not a group that will shoot from the hip. Their thought process occurs in a logical manner. You can be assured that once they have offered their feedback, their options are solidly researched and defendable. That position will stand until additional or better information is available that will justify re-visiting the matter.

How come every rush report has this warning on the bottom: "It's not that easy being Green?"

Greens are constantly thinking about one thing or another. Even a visit to the grocery store will have them standing in the line-up thinking and contemplating a number of better procedures the store should be using. They are continuously thinking through processes and improvements, probing and questioning. The best way to describe this mindset is that Greens have never met a question they didn't want to tackle.

Green Time

A great need for this group is to have a certain amount of "alone" or Green time. For others, this may be infrequent, however for Greens it is much more of a necessity, and more frequently needed. They require this for their independent processing and thinking time.

The Green mind can be compared to that of a computer, which needs regular times to do backups. It is the time when they can think things through or simply process their day in some logical fashion. While others may judge this as anti-social, for Greens it is invaluable, and is something they cannot do without. It may mean working on some project in the garage, or very often it is spending time on their computer.

When it comes to parties and social functions, Greens enjoy them as much as anyone else, but for limited periods of time. After a number of hours, their energy level drains in this environment and they frequently move to the outside of the room. While others may wonder what's wrong, Greens are still enjoying themselves immensely. They just don't wish to stay in the middle of the action, but are very content watching people from the sidelines.

The Big Picture

The preference for Greens is to first look at the big

The Color that has the most difficult time understanding alone-time are their Blue friends. It is not something Blues seek, making it difficult to relate to this strong need of high Greens. There is nothing wrong, it is just an integral part of a Greens' day.

picture. They value starting with a broad overview, then filling in details with thorough and accurate information. Even when they are only involved with specific sections, Greens will ask many detailed and probing questions to gain an understanding of how their piece fits into the big picture. Few things please Greens more than to be able to visualize something and consider all the angles, obstacles, and possibilities. Then, and only then, will they be able to execute in a logical and almost fail-safe manner. The opportunity to take something from concept to final result is an almost perfect scenario for this group.

Greens want to see the big picture first. They value the details and specifics, but start with an overview. When they have this, they are able to better comprehend their part in the process and start thinking of ways to improve and perfect the system.

Interacting with Others

A challenge for others is often wondering whether the Green person they are talking with is really listening. Frequently, they will display a *Green face*, which is really just a neutral expression or poker face. Others can view this as being cold or not listening, but nothing could be further from the truth. Greens are not generally active listeners. In their mind, the computer is on and the notebook is open. They are absorbing the information and are generally better listeners than many others.

Communicating with Greens will be more like a tennis match. The ball is in your court, now you talk. Then there will be a couple of seconds delay while they process the information and respond with few words, yet well phrased and well thought out.

Greens strongly value character and credibility for themselves and look for it in others. Communicating with them is best done when the conversations focus on logic and facts. They prefer conversations that are well articulated, concise, and to the point. Any excess of emotional talk or visual displays can quickly have Greens out of their comfort zone and tuning out.

Greens prefer communicating by e-mail. It allows them time to think the issues through and reply on their schedule. Make sure that everything in your e-mails is spelled correctly and grammatically correct. It is one of the many things they look for in judging the credibility in people, presentations, and processes.

Just say No

Greens are frequently accused that their favorite word is "no." They strive making proper and correct decisions that are well thought out and justifiable. When they are pressed into immediate answers, they often reply with a simple "no." What this actually translates to is: "if you want an answer right now before I can think about it, then it is no."

Meaningful and important questions require time to formulate correct answers. Asking this group to come up with complex solutions *off the top of their heads* will not elicit a response. That is part of the reason Greens often find themselves shaking their heads in meetings. At times when decisions are made without much thought, they simply view the whole thing as a waste of time.

Greens strive to make correct and well thought-out decisions. Then, and only then, will they give others their input.

Honoring Greens through building in that time generally results in well-informed feedback and decision-making. It also elicits a more frequent positive response. Others simply need to re-phrase their questions with this in mind.

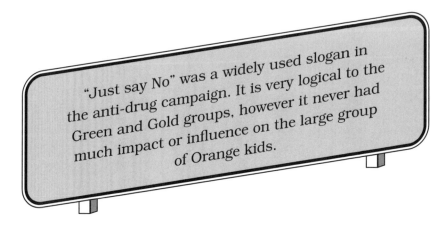

"Just say No" was a widely used slogan in the anti-drug campaign. It is very logical to the Green and Gold groups, however it never had much impact or influence on the large group of Orange kids.

Dean and a friend own a large fitness chain – a very high Orange business. Fortunately, Dean and his partner are both high Orange. An understanding of their personalities has long since caused them to hire Steve, a Green controller. He handles banking, finance, legal, and all the daily functions that aren't fun for most Oranges. Almost every morning Dean would burst into Steve's office with little slips of paper, a virtual waterfall of ideas off the top of his head and tons of questions in a typical Orange rapid-fire approach. It was driving Steve nuts, while Dean was convinced his controller was in a constant bad mood.

It was after a Colors seminar that it became clear to Dean that his controller's mood was simply caused by his Orange behavior. He perceived his quick questions, rapidly changing tracks, and many Orange ideas as positives, and expected Steve to instantly react and offer feedback. Steve, however, always became apprehensive whenever this Orange tornado hit his office. Dean had always known the value of his Green controller, but now understood that Steve would only ever supply feedback and information that was correct, well thought out, and justified. He has learned to send Steve an e-mail, a note, or rattle off his thoughts on voice-mail and arrange to meet at the end of the day. It wasn't easy, but it created a vastly improved relationship when he allowed his controller to work on his strengths, instead of pressing him for instant answers.

The Drive for Perfection

The Green mindset constantly strives for perfection. The same way they are driven to learn and grow, they look to improve procedures and processes. Hence their great frustration when they suggest improvements and others won't listen, or don't follow their suggestions. Greens certainly understand that perfection is a constantly moving target in any area of life, which is fine with them. It is the challenge of attainment that appeals to them, just as much as the actual achievement.

Once something is learned and mastered, they prefer to move on to the next challenge. Routines and not being mentally challenged are of little interest. As a result, they are always open to new and innovative ideas and quickly embrace technological changes. That is the reason this group readily purchases the latest and greatest computers, software, palm pilots, and many other electronic items.

Greens prefer to be pro-active. Do not hit them up with a number of ideas at once, expecting instant decisions and feedback. Honor them with the chance to weigh the consequences and options, to research things, and to make it perfect before they supply feedback or answers.

Selling to Greens

It is fair to say that is almost impossible to actually sell something to a Green. At best, it is a daunting task when any salesperson meets a high Green. For most of them, shopping is a task to complete and is not perceived as a pleasure.

For all larger purchases, Greens have already done their homework well in advance. They value doing this without interference and on their own time. This frequently means through the Internet. When they make a trip to the store it is most likely to obtain information they haven't otherwise been able to gather. Seldom will they make a decision right then and there, making sales staff their suppliers of information instead. To be successful with Green customers, sales people need to stay credible and very well informed.

Sales staff needs to show flexibility, and be prepared to answer a lot of technical and detailed questions that supply factual information without pressing for the sale. When that happens, there is a good chance the Green customer will return. Should the sales staff attempt to pressure or bluff, the Green customer will simply leave. When they are ready to buy, the only things Greens require are a clerk and cash register to take their money. Everything leading up to that has been done on their own, and they wouldn't have it any other way.

Never attempt to bluff Greens. Their strong desire to know and to learn means they may know more about the subject or product than you do. Even when they are ready to purchase, they will ask one or two questions where they already know the answer, simply to test the person's credibility. Bluffing your way through an answer guarantees they will walk and never return.

Even retailers have now identified high Green shoppers. Well, they are not really shoppers, but rather investigators.

Research trips focus on separating hype from reality, but avoiding salespeople whose information is obviously biased, likely inaccurate and who have little credibility. The New York based trend-watching firm Euro RSCG Worldwide has even given Greens a name, calling them prosumers. An Ottawa Citizen article describes them as "people who will have diagnosed themselves with the help of the Internet before walking into the doctor's office with their research on treatment options." Yes, of course, would be the Green response. However, retailers still have not learned how to deal with high Greens, nor understand that major purchases can well take six months or more of research.

I agree we want the perfect computer system. But it's our first anniversary, we should really get it soon...

Green Discussions

Their preferred workplace environment emulates teams of scientists or the way many I.T. firms operate. It includes having their own quiet area, but also an open environment with many others who share their values and love intricate discussions. Their rapid fire, direct or blunt questions often intimidate others, while it really should be quite the opposite. Greens only seriously pursue discussions when they have judged someone as having credibility. So it is actually a compliment when Greens want to get into a good debate or discussion.

This does not come from a mindset of criticism. They are not looking for ways to shoot down suggestions, recommendations, or find fault. Greens asking questions is simply an effort for them to gain a more in-depth understanding. The more information is shared with them, the more they will be able to provide valuable feedback, or help with finding inconsistencies and weaknesses. In those circumstances, they can also become fixer to others that may just want to be heard. It is only logical for them to interject solutions to something they may view as quite simple. Rather than jumping into defensive mode, others need to be cognizant and receptive to the conversation style of their Green friends. It is important to understand that Green feedback is not criticism. When a high Green corrects, comments or points out errors, it is always from a mindset of giving better information.

Greens have a strong dislike in repeating themselves. Greens believe once they have stated something it should stand until it needs to be revised. That applies to processes as much as comments and affirmations.

Calm, Cool and Collected

This is one of the best descriptions to fit this group. It is their general demeanor, as well as their listening style. Others can often view this as cold or unemotional, however it is their consistent manner in almost any circumstance.

In that same vein, decisions are not based on emotions or feelings. They are made from the head, and involve rational thinking and logic. This group does not readily show emotions. They feel, hurt, and care just as deeply as anyone else, but prefer to internalize their feelings through the filter of logic and their minds. Logic for many Greens also means they will have no interest in watching animated movies as animals that talk is simply silly. Many don't even have enjoy fresh cut flowers – flowers that are dead as they often call these. "Well, they're not dead now, but it's just a matter of time."

No, when they said you had a "Green face" they weren't talking about anything medical.

Recognizing a Green

You can spot high Greens in some basic ways. They'll speak in few words and have a very calm, cool, and collected demeanor. Often others will feel they're being evaluated when they first interact with a Green. Seldom will Greens show visible emotions, coming across as reserved and cool. What to wear is not of great importance, as clothing is a necessity and not worn to impress anyone. They often own the latest gadgets, computers or palm pilots, while their workspace can be quite messy or unorganized, and you'll see many books or manuals.

When you're listening to them, you will often get lots of questions, frequently asking "why" and "how." They can show annoyance at being asked to repeat things, and they will give logical, direct, and specific answers. Greens are people of few words, but they will be well chosen. Greens also take the time to think through a question before answering, so it won't be an instant response. They will often use clever humor or sarcasm and express themselves in terms of "I think" instead of "I feel."

Now I Understand...

Your need for Green time each day is not about me. It is not about being anti-social. It is time you reserve, and need, just for yourself.

Before I press you for an instant response, I should decide if I really need an answer now, or whether I value your well thought out responses.

You think things through properly and do nothing half-baked. You look at the big picture and weigh all the options and possibilities. You take the time to see the whole puzzle while I may just be seeing a box of pieces.

With your easy-going nature, your feelings do run deep. Just because they don't always come to the surface does not mean they aren't real or don't exist.

I appreciate spending time with you, and it's not only about talking all the time. Sometimes the best communication with you is when you say nothing at all – just your calm strength, logic, and demeanor.

Your Green face is not a way to measure your listening skills, or a scale to judge how much you care. Behind it is a great amount of caring and an ability to listen to me.

When you ask me a lot of questions, it is not a criticism of what I've said. It's your never-ending desire to know more and more. It is not a reason for me to become defensive, but an honor that you value learning something from me.

I am your boss or your friend. I am your partner, someone you work with or your relative and now I understand you a little better.

Common Strengths

Analytical & logical	Calm, cool & collected
Creative	Credibility
Curiosity rules	Don't need to be monitored
Enjoy our own company	Enjoys solitude
Focus on important things	Future oriented
Great problem solvers	Honest & direct
Independent & self-directed	Ingenuity
Innovative	Inquisitive
Knowing the questions to ask	Knowledgeable
Learning & teaching others	Logical
No question we won't tackle	Not overly emotional
Perfectionists & high standards	Power to ask "what if"
Problem solvers	Rational
Self-confident	Sense of humor
Skeptical	Take nothing for granted
Theoretical	To the point
Visionaries	Well-read
Wide variety of interests	

Common Stresses

Anticipate problems

Emotional outbursts

Incompetence – self & others

Insufficient information

Intrusion into our
comfort zone

Meetings with no point

No challenge/too
much repetition

Not knowing or understanding

Others who don't
value learning

Pushy sales people

Relying on other's
thought process

Spelling & grammatical errors

Things not working the way
they are supposed to

Unjust things

Worrying about forgetting something

Deadlines

Forgetting something

Inefficiencies

Interruptions

Know we're right
and others don't believe it

No time & not enough alone time

Noise

Others bluffing us

People in the way of strategy

Quick decisions

Rules that don't make sense

Stupid rules & too many
restrictions

Things that don't make sense

Welfare mindset

Chapter 7

Those Other Colors

Fortunately, nobody lives only in their primary Color. It would make relating to others a lot easier, but would also make us very one-dimensional. People function in many different ways, at different times and circumstances. For many, just the way they *need* to act at work may be quite different from how they *want* to act at home.

For all of us, our second Color plays a large roll in many behaviors and action. It is commonly referred to as the *shadow* Color. This is the part of our personality that lies in the shadow of the primary motivators or strengths, but still plays a powerful role in shaping our values, behaviors and life.

We are not unique in our primary Color. What makes us different and special are the various combinations. Our first Color is akin to having a mono radio, turned on full volume. The second Color is like adding surround sound and a volume control. These very much govern and influence the actions, thoughts, and behaviors of our primary Color.

Only a small percentage of the population is well balanced in all their four Colors. Most people tend to function in their strongest (primary) and second (shadow) Colors. Unlike Punxsutawney Phil, the shadow Color does come out more often than once a year. It is more akin to being permanently *shadowed*. How strongly it influences their life and actions varies from person to person.

It is the joy of having the other three Colors that really makes everyone much more special and unique. Like a jigsaw puzzle, a complete person has each of the four Color pieces present in their life. However, they frequently come in much different sizes which contributes to diversity, uniqueness, and depth of character. It also significantly increases the complexities of both understanding others and ourselves.

To make matters more confusing, not everyone with the same primary Color is identical. Not to mention the rich diversity created when a whole list of secondary factors is taken into consideration. Just looking at the first two Colors makes for many unique combinations – some more common, and others much more infrequent.

Curt is a Blue/Gold Pastor. His first career after graduation was in the construction industry. The one thing that always horrified him was any project that did not have a complete set of blueprints. His high Gold and very low Orange did not want to just *wing it*, but needed clear and specific instructions. Even without knowing his Colors, Curt always knew in the back of his mind that he had this driving need to pursue more of a people-oriented career. As a strong Christian and active member of his church, he soon realized his true calling was to be a Pastor.

The years at seminary were both richly rewarding and painfully difficult. His Blue instinctively knew that this was his true purpose in life. Likewise, with his high Gold, the thought of quitting before graduating almost never entered his mind. When he received his calling to a congregation, Curt's primary job description was leading the various youth groups and taking charge of the Sunday school. Using his planning and organizational skills, he was always prepared. From candy to activities, from stories to fun and games, the kids and their parents adored him. While Curt's Blue loved working with people, the talents needed for high Orange kids are quite different than those required in working with adults. His strong core strengths of duty and serving were conflicting with his desire to grow and work in a lesser Orange area of the church. That opportunity was not possible in that particular congregation. Today Curt is Dean of Residence to over two hundred students at a very large Bible College. Finally, a position which fully utilizes his Gold/Blue strengths.

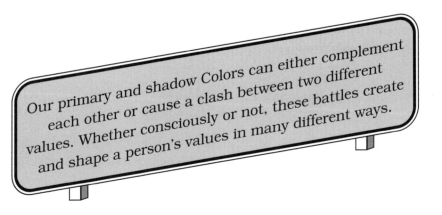

Our primary and shadow Colors can either complement each other or cause a clash between two different values. Whether consciously or not, these battles create and shape a person's values in many different ways.

Time and again, everyone's mind weighs the consequences of one action over another. To what degree one or the other dominates depends on how strong the shadow Color is, or how important the decision being made. There are times when the primary Color will lose out to a degree.

A Gold/Green will often limit their search for more information to achieve closure and put something behind them. Another example is a high Orange/Blue. While the need for competition and winning is always in existence, when it comes to competitive sports for example, they will often stop short of actions or comments which hurt others. That simply honors their high Blue values, which is also a dominant part of their personality.

If there is a genuine desire to grow and learn, it necessitates doing things a little differently. A good place to start is with a hard look at your last Color. They are not your strengths, but they are the life of others. Perhaps doing something different means just withholding judgment of them at times. Keep in mind these are the big strengths and values of others. Other people, whose life is lived in your last Color, are the hardest to relate to. It is the group that definitely presses your buttons in their behavior, actions, and many other ways.

The Different View of Others

We often see each other in drastically different ways. The chart below explains some of these different views. It compares how we think of ourselves, but also how others might see us when looking at some actions or behaviors through totally different eyes.

Blue may see itself as	Others may see Blue as
Affirming others	A push-over & too nice
Compassionate	Bleeding heart
Creative	Can't see the real world
Empathetic	Easily taken advantage of
Great communicator	Mushy
Idealistic	Naïve
Likes to please	Not task oriented & gets sidetracked
People person	Overly emotional
Romantic	Smothering
Social interactions	Soft hearted
Spiritual	Sugar-coats things
Trusting	Talks too much
Wants harmony	Too trusting or soft
Warm & caring	Unrealistic

Perhaps we are actually three different people.
The way we see ourselves, how others see us and the way we really are.

Gold may see itself as

Abides by policies

Always has a view

Business type

Can be counted on

Decisive

Efficient

Dependable

Goal oriented

Great planner

Orderly & neat

Practical and stable

Provides security

Realistic

Steady & firm

Very organized

Others may see Gold as

Black or white & one-tracked

Bossy

Controlling

Controls & sets own agenda

Dull or boring

End justifies the means

Judgmental

Limited flexibility

No imagination

Opinionated

Predictable

Rigid & often only their way

Stubborn

Stuck in the system

Uptight

Green may see itself as

Able to reprimand

Always right 97% of the time

Calm under pressure

Creative

Efficient

Exact, not repetitive

Firm minded

Logical decisions

Rational

Seeking justice

Superior intellectually

Thinking it through

Tough minded

Unique and original

Others may see Green as

Aloof & cool

Arrogant

Cold

Controlled

Doesn't care about people

Finding fault

Hatchet person

Heartless

Intellectual snob

Lacks mercy & caring

Not involved in team

Ruthless

Unfeeling & aloof

Unrealistic

Orange may see itself as	Others may see Orange as
Doesn't get stressed	Always late & off track
Enjoys life	Can't be taken seriously
Flexible	Disobeys rules
Fun loving	Doesn't get focused
Great negotiator	Doesn't know right from wrong
Here and now person	Flaky
Multi-tasking	Irresponsible
New ideas & suggestions	Manipulator
Practical	Problem creator
Problem solver	Shortcuts systems & rule breaker
Resourceful	Tramples over others
Spontaneous	Vague and can't be justified
Winning attitude	Won't follow the plan

Perhaps anything taken to an extreme can be too much of a good thing. Are there any strengths that you sometimes take too far? While each Color has many things they're really good at, when taken to an extreme, it has a noticeable effect on others. Living in balance means understanding that moderation is always the key.

That was the great thing learning about Colors. One group says no a lot. One group can't say no at all and another doesn't even hear the word no.

"Many actions you take have a reaction in others – many more than you realize."

For Golds, it can be an understanding that not everything has to be planned and it is not wise to force others to be on time, every time. For the Orange group, it may be the challenge to sometimes focus on one thing at a time and to stay serious more often around certain people. Perhaps the consistent Green trait of being calm, cool, and collected has turned to cold in the eyes of others. Or maybe Blue's steadfast strength of living in their heart has others challenged to find a way to communicate in factual and logical terms from time to time.

We all have a volume control we can use. Any strengths, when taken over the top, can quickly become a problem in our life. Organizing can become controlling and create added stress. Alone time can become anti-social. Giving into others can lead to being taken advantage of and mistreated. Or perhaps the strength of multi-tasking can cause missed deadlines and sales.

Perception sometimes is reality. Since no one lives life in isolation, what others think or feel is worth contemplating. Looking in the mirror sometimes means taking that feedback into account. Are all your strengths, or letting many of your stresses show, getting you more of what you want in the big picture of life?

"In every journey there is a purpose.
In every stress there is opportunity for growth.
In every conflict, there is a lesson.
In every team there is strength in all Colors.
In every relationship there are differences.
In every action, there is a choice.

In everyone's difference there is value.
In every other person there is a unique individual.
In every strength there is joy.
In every behavior there is an option.
In every comfort zone there is a missed chance for growth.

In every Color there is beauty.
In every primary Color there is comfort and safety.
In every shadow Color there is time of conflict.
In every pale Color there is a chance to practice.
In every moment of doubt, remember to believe in yourself."

Understanding others and their personality differences begins with looking for the value. Every day, we judge many other people in less than a minute. We judge them based on our own criteria and values and see them through our own set of glasses. If you believe that people come into your life for a reason, you're ahead of the game already. Is our first reaction that they are cold and aloof, for instance? Or are we prepared to consider that they may instead be seen as calm, cool and collected?

If you meet a high Orange person, full of energy, running late, and talking very quickly, what's your first thought? What about those at work focused intensely on their current project at hand? Do we view them as uncaring and totally task-oriented? Or are we prepared to view things slightly differently and see them as focused and getting the job done? Last, but not least, do we perceive our Blue friends as always making time for others and genuinely caring about those around them? Or is our initial reaction in the office that there is too much talk and not enough work?

> The lowest Color of your personality will be the people in your life that you have the most difficulty relating to. It will be the chapter that seems to go on forever, as the insights about this group are so foreign to you. Yet this is the area where you will learn the most.

The challenge is to re-read the chapter of your pale, or last Color. Many times in life, the biggest hurdles will be dealing with others whose life is in that Color. Whether it is in the office, with in-laws or friends, these *opposites* will naturally have the largest personality differences from you. Hence, they are the people in your life that you will have the most challenge in understanding and relating to.

> *"I judge a man by the gold on the inside.*
> *I'm not fooled by the glitter on the outside.*
> *It ain't how far you go, it's not how much you make.*
> *It's being strong and true to those counting on you."*
> Kevin Sharp

Our Common Denominators

Before looking to our differences, there are any number of things our Colors have in common. Here are just some of these:

Blue and Orange
These two are both very people-oriented personalities that value their time and interaction with others. People definitely come ahead of paperwork. They both automatically default to always looking at the positives and bright side of things.

They are naturally optimistic and look first for the good in others. Both seek recognition and shine brighter when they receive genuine positive feedback for their unique talents and contributions. They are excellent problem solvers and eternal optimists who share a natural ability to be great negotiators, although in different ways. Oranges excel through their desire to win, their ability to wing it, and by being able to think on their feet. Blues excel through their strong sense of intuition and ability to relate so well to others. Both strongly value recognition – Orange in contests, gifts, and money; Blues through genuine words of affirmation and praise – preferably in public.

Gold and Green

These are both task-oriented in their overall outlook and behavior and will generally put the job to be done ahead of people issues. Their demeanor is less friendly and more business-like and reserved. Greens tend to be calm and cool, while Golds generally have a concerned or focused demeanor. Both look at the challenges, pitfalls, and potential problems of things. They value getting things right and can focus intensely on their projects at hand, with a preference to function in terms of logic, process, and quality issues.

Green and Orange

These two love competition of one kind or another and new goals or challenges. It is the challenge to make something better, faster, or more efficient that appeals to them. This makes both rather independent in their thoughts and actions. Oranges love to compete with anyone about anything, just for the sake of competition and keeping things interesting and challenging. Greens prefer competition with themselves or with systems of some kind. Both have strong independent streaks and need their space to perform. They are both eager to seek new ways and methods of doing things – Oranges with a drive to avoid boredom and routine, and Green to improve, grow, and show society their ingenuity.

Gold and Blue

Both of these thrive on their common bond of helping and assisting others. They are generous with their money for charities and worthy causes. Both gain a large part of their self-esteem by helping, contributing, and lending a hand. To them, it is a natural drive and obligation they perform without thought. Golds tend to focus more on service clubs, their church, or other community groups. On the other hand, Blues gravitate toward helping people, animals and the less fortunate in society. For an employer, this motivation to be willing to help and assist makes them great team players in any organization.

Green and Blue

While Greens function with their head and Blues live in their hearts, these two do have some strong bonds. Their common denominators are their creativity and focus on the big picture over the details and results. Creativity to the Green is measured through growth, improving systems, and procedures. For the Blue person, it tends to be more focused toward their strength in the artistic areas.

Gold and Orange

In overall terms, these two are quite different in their behavior and preferences. Their strong bond is the ability to work well as a team – Golds with their focus on helping and serving others as a sense of duty, as well as getting the job done. For Oranges, it is being people-oriented along with their high energy, enthusiasm, and flexibility in almost any situation when they are internally motivated. Both function for today and the job at hand, and do not spend much time focusing on long range plans, ideas, or visions. They also share an impatient streak in many areas of life.

*"Always spend more time looking for what
you have in common than looking
for the differences"*

Oranges and Blues are people first Colors and soft on people. Golds and Greens are task first Colors – hard on tasks.

Changing the Results

> *"To have some different results*
> *you have to do some different things."*

Understanding others, while very valuable, does have it's limitations. At some point, it also needs to include a look in the mirror. An easy example for Golds and Greens is often the question of what comes first, people or tasks? Most of the time, there is agreement that it's always people first. If that is the case, why do actions often speak louder than words? Perhaps a look in the mirror involves giving some thought to looking at our challenges or behaviors.

Golds

> *"Don't push closure or force your point of view – I understand your point of view."*

For Golds, decisions on many issues are generally black or white. You possess a strong desire to get things off the list and to get on with it. This can create a mindset of wanting an answer, sometimes any answer, just to be done with it. Lingering issues and unresolved matters cause stress that can become noticeable to others. Of course, it is also true that often pushing for an answer creates exactly the opposite outcome of the one you are seeking.

The second issue for Golds are the times when you supply answers, or assert your point of view. For others, decisions do not come in only black or white. There are significant shades of gray in between these two extremes that Golds can sometimes miss. Viewpoints, like feelings do not have a right or wrong answer. The challenge might be to stay out of your judgments or *easy conclusions* and honor the other person by considering their point of view.

Blues

"Don't ever be afraid to state your needs and be strong enough to stand up for them."

As discussed in the Blue chapter, it is very difficult for you to say "no." Others, consciously or not, can take advantage of that. When everyone doesn't share your open and caring nature it can become a problem. Others can perceive you as doormats, which is also frequently how it actually feels to you.

The challenge is in standing up for your needs, or perhaps just learning to say "no" or "enough" to yourself or others. Knowing the challenge and its value, and committing to acting on it is a different matter. Nobody will think less of you, nor will they view this as selfish. Often it can be quite the opposite. People around you will respect some boundaries and will learn that giving is of more value when it becomes a two-way street. That, however, necessitates having to get out of your comfort zone to educate others, and to believe this will not jeopardize your relationship.

"All behaviors have consequences.
Positive or negative – for better or worse.
Are yours getting you more of what you want
in the big picture of life?"

Oranges

"Stick to your original specific agreements and see them through to completion."

When given a choice, seeing things through to the end can be a challenge. Deadlines are frequently a stress, since the fun is in being the idea starter or instigator and not always the finisher.

The other half of the issue becomes even more of a challenge. You love to wing it without too much preparation. You are very receptive to new ideas and better suggestions that come along, which is why you value not being firmly committed to any specific plan. When you readily change tracks or agreements, others can perceive it as not keeping your word. They may not judge this as a matter of evolving the plan, but simply as not sticking with something you have agreed to.

Greens

"Be ready, willing and able to give in sometimes, even if it doesn't make sense."

When something is not logical, the Green mind knows it. That makes it a significant obstacle to give in when your mind is screaming "no"! It becomes a problem with others and in relationships when that mindset takes over. Often this is especially true in the broad area of dealing with feelings. When emotions are involved, not many things may be logical, but they often are to others. Your sharp and intelligent mind in this example can be seen as a challenge. Something that may not be logical to you can still feel, or seem, perfectly *right* to others.

Who knows, others may well come around to your viewpoint, but with their own agenda and on their own time. A good question to ask may often be "is this the hill I want to die on?" Put another way, is this a matter worth fighting for?

Every person can think of at least a couple of behaviors, or strengths, that others have difficulty understanding when they are taken to extremes. Perhaps it is the challenge of Golds to put away their to-do lists for a weekend, or for Greens to allow others to share some of their feelings. For Oranges it may be to stay focused when others require it, or honoring their need to be on time. Perhaps for Blues it is to be cognizant of being overly emotional or taking too many things to heart that others had never intended as a personal attack.

"When you change your thinking,
You change your beliefs;
When you change your beliefs,
You change your expectations;
When you change your expectations,
You change your attitude;
When you change your attitude,
You change your behavior;
When you change your behavior,
You change your performance;
When you change your performance;
You change Your Life!"
Author unknown

What a powerful quote, and it all starts with changing some thinking.

- To have more of what works in life means making some concessions to the values of other Colors.

- Understand your strengths and become aware of which ones you can take to extremes.

- Be aware of the differences of others, the unique values and joys that are part of their personality. Understand that they will always be a part of them. Take the time to communicate and appreciate others on their terms.

- Stay aware of the things that cause you stress and how it can show to others. Not all their behaviors will make you happy, nor will many things that they say or do. Be aware of your reactions in many situations.

- Teach others what is important to you and what you are like. No one can control the actions or reactions of others, nor can we change others. We can, however, teach them what we value, desire, and look for in many areas of our life. Recognize that there is nobody that chooses to annoy you on purpose. When others understand you a little better, they will stay out of their judgments, and your relationships will improve.

Can you share with people in your life that you strongly value being on time and actually pick the important times? Do others need to understand your strong desire for freedom, movement, and staying flexible? Many people most certainly need to teach their friends to value their Green alone-time without having them assume it is an anti-social behavior. Finally, the challenge for our Blue friends to teach others their need and desire for open communication and to be included and acknowledged.

Maybe we will be off this island by Friday. It's great that you're always so reliable, but was it really necessary to kill the cell phone battery cancelling your appointments?

Gordon is a high Gold dating a high Orange woman. One of his strong personality traits is the value he places on always being on time. Dating Jennifer made that a large challenge. She certainly did not share that need and it became a significant issue in their relationship. When Gordon understood the differences in their view of time management, he realized there were only two options.

One choice was to keep trying to nag or educate his Orange girlfriend, hoping that she would change and come around to his way of thinking. He quickly realized that this would never meet with much success. Instead, he chose to have an honest look at his need to always be on time, and to define those occasions important to him, instead of it just being desired. When he sat down with Jennifer, he shared his distinction between wanting to be on time and needing to be on time. Gordon explained to her that he had to be on time when it involved meeting others or attending church. In return, he learned to embrace Jennifer's ability to constantly be on the go, and her ability to multi-task, which often caused her to run late. When he understood that there was no real need to be on time for a party, sporting event, or many others occasions, his relationship drastically improved. In turn, Jennifer readily understood and honored his needs for the important occasions.

With those small steps in helping others understand us better, we can truly embrace the rainbow of differences and their special values in creating balance in our life, home, and workplace. The alternative is fighting the behavior of others, or jumping into our judgments, neither of which ever gets us more of what we want in life.

"You need to have a plan ahead of time.
Our behaviors and reaction to others have trigger points.
There are times when they will seep through or
even blow up."

So can you flex or stretch today? Can you do something today that is a little out of your comfort zone? The challenge is to do one thing a little differently every day. It needs to be small enough that you'll do it, but large enough that you'll notice. Perhaps it starts with looking at others in your life a little differently. Perhaps looking at them as gifts:

Persons are Gifts
Persons are gifts of God to me. They are already wrapped.
Some beautifully and others less attractively.
Some have been mishandled in the mail, others come
"special delivery", some are loosely wrapped, and others
very tightly enclosed.

*But the wrapping is not the gift and this is an important
realization. It is so easy to make a mistake in this regard,
to judge the contents by the cover.
Sometimes the gift is opened very easily; sometimes
the help of others is needed. Maybe it is because they
are afraid to look inside my wrapping. Maybe I don't
trust my own contents.
Or it may be that I have never fully accepted
the gift that I am.
Every meeting and sharing of persons is an
exchange of gifts.
My gift is Me; your gift is You.
We are gifts to each other.*
Author unknown

Who are You Where?

Do you really love your job? If so, it probably means you
are working in an environment and job that strongly matches
your primary personality.

What part of your personality comes out the strongest
when you are at home? With your partner, kids, or family do
you utilize a different part of your personality in those
circumstances? Most people readily admit they want to be
balanced in their life, while retaining all the strengths of their
primary Color that are so comfortable and valued. There are
times for everyone to get organized and stick to a plan, or to
just let loose and have fun. Times to let others into our hearts
share our feelings or to just get a warm hug. Or other times
when it is important to think things through, perhaps by
stepping back to look at the big picture and logically gathering
all the information needed to make a good decision.

Striving for Balance

To focus only on the strengths in our personalities
does not result in being well balanced. While it is very easy
to do, and quite natural, focusing on our other Colors takes
a little more effort. If balance does not come naturally, it can
certainly be accomplished in our behavior. Perhaps living in
balance means:

Your **Green** pursues challenges and solutions, constantly seeking improvements, and keeping your eye on the big picture and broader visions. Your range of knowledge goes far beyond your job, and it is well known and respected. You enjoy research, learning and growing, continuously looking for opportunities to share your broad knowledge and well thought out ideas and suggestions with others.

Your **Blue** consistently shows in you caring for others, and reaching out to them. You involve everyone around you and give from the heart – to your friends, family and others. Your kindness and communication skills touch everyone you come into contact with. Your genuine warmth, empathy, and teamwork skills are contagious and impact those around you. You make lasting friendships and are always ready, willing, and able to make time for others.

Your **Gold** stands out in your loyalty, dependability, and special talents to take on tasks and see them through to completion. Your strong sense of right and wrong, work ethic, and planning are qualities others appreciate. Your word is always good and you function well to deadlines without supervision. You work at the same time as both an individual and as a team players, and people can always count on you to pitch in wherever and whenever you are needed.

We use all four Colors in our life every day. But not to the same degree. From an early age in life most of us have begun to rely on one or two primary Colors.

*Your **Orange** is the energy and positive outlook that everyone admires. You have a contagious sense of humor and teach others that anything is possible through your practical actions, and high energy level. Your ability to multi-task and your gift of flexibility, without stress, is valued and envied by those that watch you in action. You are never afraid to roll up your sleeves and get involved in practical and creative ways that only you can pull off.*

Or to summarize:

Embrace yourself as you are...

Just for today –
Make your Gold lists shorter,
Nurture your Blue relationships,
Value and grow your Green knowledge
And treasure your Orange freedom.

Chapter 8

Relationships

Is it true that the motto for relationships might be that opposites attract? It is likely that this initially attracts us to others who appear quite different from our personality.

In the feedback received from large groups of participants, the responses bear that out. The attendees were asked to list their primary Color and that of their partner or significant other. It should be noted that these results are certainly not scientific. In fact, it may well be that the odd participant even misjudged the primary Color of their partner. The results however are significant enough numbers to merit consideration.

Primary Color	Partner's Primary Color			
	Gold	Orange	Blue	Green
Gold	23%	25%	24%	28%
Orange	45%	15%	19%	21%
Blue	20%	27%	19%	34%
Green	39%	18%	37%	6%

Of the Gold participants, fully 25 percent are in a relationship with an Orange partner, and 45 percent of the Orange respondents with a Gold partner. In similarly large numbers, one-third of Blues are attracted to a high Green partner. This is certainly some direct proof of the saying that opposites do attract.

At first it may be very appealing to find different characteristics in others that we may lack. Most dating relationships, however start with what is sometimes called the *pink-lens effect*. This is certainly present in the courtship stages of the initial self-disclosure period and the *can't be apart* stage. It begins through filtering out someone's negative traits, building up their positive side, and easily explaining away their flaws. As time goes by and the relationship matures, some of those personality traits can also start wearing a little thin. As an example, the original attraction of a super-organized partner, always on time and very determined, can also turn to being viewed as rigid and a little stubborn.

"Maybe God wants us to meet a few wrong people before meeting the right one. So that when we finally meet the right person, we will know how to be grateful for that gift."
Author unknown

Whom do you date or marry? Challenges can arise in any relationship, regardless of your partner's Color. Will you remember the awesome traits that you were first attracted to? Will you remember them down the road and still value them? If that is the case, love is always colorblind.

At times, the relationship may well turn to spending energy making the other person more like us. It becomes a slippery slope when one partner makes an effort to "fix" the other's traits or behaviors.

The next step is where conflict first arises. It is the period where the first arguments start and each partner is now actually contemplating some initial negative thoughts.

Ok, maybe I will go out with you. We're quite different, but after I gave you my wrong name and phone number you still found me!

The original appeal of calm, cool, collected, and logical can also turn to being thought of as cold, unfeeling, and uncaring. Likewise, a strong Orange personality with their positive outlook, high energy, and multi-tasking nature might one day be seen as unrealistic or irresponsible. As the old expression says "beauty is in the eye of the beholder." This also applies to personality types – different views for different people, and from very different perspectives. It always depends on who does the judging.

Friendships, on the other hand, generally start with common experiences or shared values. A larger circle of friends also includes people with different strengths, values, or views on life. It is through a varied circle of friends that individuals grow and learn, and have others in their life who challenge their comfort zones or are there at just the right times, in their own special way.

Relationships require hard work, the ability to communicate well, and many other tools and building blocks to make them successful. Knowing Colors is not a dating tool, but it does create an understanding of personality strengths, stresses and values. What do you want out of the relationship? What traits do you most admire in a person? What character issues are of great value to you? What creates a real stress for you in the actions or behaviors of others?

It is important to remember that each of us is a combination of all four personality parts, or Colors. That means dating is not about finding someone who has only one of these pieces. Fortunately, everyone is a unique blend of many personality traits and to varying degrees.

Communication is recognized as the main building block of any successful relationship. Along with every Color's desire for time spent together, communication is the most frequently mentioned factor contributing to the strengthening or coming apart of a relationship. If communication is one of the key factors, it is also a prime area of conflict. This is most noticeable when relationships involve different primary Colors. When they are the same, effective communication comes more naturally. When two partners are different Colors, it means more work and effort is required to achieve effective communication.

Understand and appreciate your partner for who they really are, not for what they could be. It is a positive way to nurture and grow the relationship. Celebrate your differences. Attempting to change the other person only builds resentment, defensiveness and stress.

Celebrate each other's contribution to the relationship and focus on the big picture instead of the little things that can annoy you. Keep in mind the many times and special ways others are there for you and help you grow. Think of the many positive things they contribute to enriching your life.

Relationship Challenges

There are also some common challenges that each Color group can exhibit. Here are three specific ones to consider in order to strengthen any relationship:

No relationship is ever a 50–50 proposition. That is just the divorce rate! It is always 100%–100% work by both partners. It is always about balance, which begins inside each of us and extends to all our relationships. It starts with an attitude of looking for the value in those around us each and every day.

For Oranges

Oranges add variety and excitement to any relationship. They are generous, action-oriented, and eternal optimists. Their drive for freedom means Oranges can have a tendency to give up on a relationship when they start feeling tied down.

- Not everything is fun. One of your challenges is that others may not take you seriously when you really want to be. The ease with which you can switch back and forth is not one that many others can do and thus they find it difficult to keep up, or to recognize when you have switched gears.

- Fight fair. Your big desire is to be a winner, something to remember when you argue or fight in a relationship. Those may not be the times to win at all costs. Sometimes your partner wants to discuss, argue or fight about something specific. Honor them by focusing on that subject. You can make fights really nasty and quickly get side-tracked. It might just drag out the fight and make it bigger for no reason. When it comes to others you care about, is it really important that they lose and you win? Will it not just be a lose-lose situation by the time the fight is over anyway?

- Hang in there more often. Let's be honest, you like things fast and immediate. In relationships, that can become an issue. When things aren't going well, you can have a tendency to quit. In the early stages, you sometimes have to be a little patient, as not everyone moves at your pace. You frequently have that nagging feeling that there is something missing. The feeling that there may be something *more* out there beyond being *tied-down* as you perceive it. Sometimes it's important to think it through before voting with your feet.

When in doubt – use humor! Laughter truly is one of the best medicines. It actually aids to stimulate the immune system and acts as nature's great stress reliever. It's also in the top three most attractive characteristics others look for in their partner!

For Greens

Greens value knowledge and intelligence in relationships just as much as the rest of life. Their prime interest is not in the romantic, or the emotional aspects of relationships. They are very serious and careful in selecting their partner for that reason. One of the first considerations in their choice of a partner is someone who is able to keep up mentally, and is a match for their intelligence level.

- Speak from the heart. Yes, it may be difficult to talk about feelings. It is, however, of great importance to the large majority of the population. After all, high Blues always value talking about feelings and communicating from the heart. Share with those closest to you how you feel and allow them to see a little piece of your heart. It contributes greatly to strengthened relationships and brings you closer together. Besides, what's the worst that can happen?

- Calm, cool, and collected is sometimes difficult for others to understand. They do value your calm demeanor in many situations. But there are times when people close to you would like to see the caring, warm, and gentle side. It will create stronger bonds when you trust those you care about enough to let them see your other or hidden side.

- Teach others the meaning of *Green time*. You need some alone time every day. Rather than simply fading away, teach those you care about what your needs are. This is your time to unwind and process your day. Often others think it means you are anti-social, and it hurts their feelings. When they understand why you treasure this time, it has a measurable impact and brings you closer together. Think about it – others don't need or understand it, so it is up to you to educate them.

For Golds

This group tends to take any relationship very seriously. They prefer traditional dating methods and old-fashioned courtship. They do many things out of a sense of duty and are very loyal friends and partners. During the dating process, they are fully committed and can be off their agenda. That situation generally does not last forever. At some point, it is the tendency of Golds to get back to their sense of duty and focus on the tasks at hand. To Golds it becomes a situation of getting back to equilibrium in their life. To others it can be viewed as taking the relationship for granted.

- Put aside your agenda. Sometimes it's OK just to go with the flow. You believe that changing plans or arrangements isn't right. When your partner has a change of heart, you can honor them by going along with their wishes. Who knows, it might expose you to something new and interesting if you remain flexible and open-minded. If not, it will show your inflexibility to work together as a team.

- Understand that not everyone shares your strong desire to be on time, every time. When others rely on you, being on time is simply common courtesy. Does that need to include being exactly on time for a movie, party, or concert? What's the worst that can happen if you're not? You'd miss the previews or ten minutes of a warm-up band? In return for *forcing* your partner to stay on time, you've created stress and tension for no reason. Communicate honestly and openly that being on time is important for specific times, and compromise by not making it an issue worth fighting over every day.

If we want this relationship to work, we'll have to get organized. So we'll hold hands from 8:30 until 8:45 and then we'll have small talk for 14 minutes...

- Recognize that others can view all kinds of issues in shades of gray. For Golds, most things are black or white, right or wrong. For better or worse, that perspective is not shared by the entire world. Be ready and willing to look at some things from more of a gray perspective. Consider the old saying that there are two sides to every story, with the truth somewhere in between. After all, wouldn't you rather be happy than right?

For Blues

This group is the relationship specialist of the four Colors. However, they can reach a sense of disappointment if their dreams of the perfect relationship are not fulfilled. They can also develop a sense of impending doom in their thoughts that "it can't stay this good forever..."

- Understand when it's not about you. That is easier said than done. You wear your heart on your sleeve and turning off your emotions is not possible. Frequently, when your partner says or does certain things, your first reaction is that it is about you. How often has someone not acknowledged your greetings? Isn't the first thing that goes through your mind that you've done something to make them mad? How often has it turned out that it was not about you at all?

- Your best is all you have. What really hurts is the feelings deep down that you haven't done enough. Whenever you lend a hand that is often how you feel. In each situation, you can only give 100 percent and nothing more. When you truly believe that, it will show in your demeanor, self-confidence, and the way you feel about yourself.

- Look after yourself first. Selfish as that may sound, the alternative is that run-down feeling that you have often experienced. It might mean saying no at times, and setting boundaries. You will be much stronger, healthier, and better able to reach out to others when you have first taken care of yourself. It will create a big impact for you, and will be easily noticed by those you care about.

Take a rubber band and pull it apart with both your hands. How long can you hold it that way? What happens when you let it go? That is how long and how likely it is to change the personality of your partner. Celebrate your differences, value them for who they are, and remember these were the same traits that first attracted you to them.

Since the arenas of professional sports and acting are prime careers for many Oranges, no discussion of relationships would be complete without a look at Hollywood.

Nicolas Cage divorced Lisa Marie Presley within three months. Drew Barrymore married bar owner Jeremy Thomas for all of 19 days in 1976, but in 2000 did make her marriage to Tom Green last five full months. Not really funny is it? Stories quoted Green as not being able to adjust to her "liberated ways."

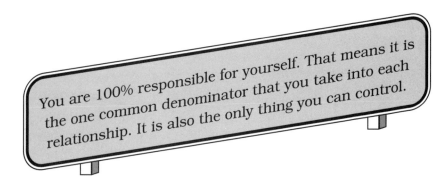

You are 100% responsible for yourself. That means it is the one common denominator that you take into each relationship. It is also the only thing you can control.

Marriage counselors acknowledge that the first year of marriage is the most challenging. Built into that time frame is the assumption that there has at least been some extensive dating. Michelle Phillips (ex of the Mamas & Papas) lasted eight days with actor Dennis Hopper. In her words, "It was the happiest eight days of my life." But then, Britney Spears barely lasted two days before having her Vegas marriage annulled, only to remarry nine months later. Pamela Anderson married rocker Tommy Lee after having known him for four days, and her first filing for divorce was within a year. Then there is another power couple in Angeline Jolie and Billy Bob Thornton. Their marriage lasted almost two years, although Jolie states things started to unravel as soon as they moved in together. It was her second marriage and his fifth. Practice does not seem to make perfect.

Without presuming to judge their Colors, some of these well-known personalities are certainly high Orange. Quick decision-making is a great strength for them. However, when it comes to making marriage decisions on that same basis, it comes with great risks. Having a total belief that they can pull off anything is a double-edged sword. Without a doubt, that belief and personality trait has gotten these people (whether high Orange or not) to the pinnacle of their professions. On the other hand, some also believe that they can take that same talent into a making a relationship work, often against all odds.

The commonly heard themes for failures in relationships are as varied as the personalities involved. An often-heard area of dispute is where one partner wants some significant life change more than the other. Should that involve asking their partner to move across the country or to work less? Good luck asking that of an Orange who lives for their work, is the center of attention, paid very well, and has entire studios catering to their needs and desires.

> Orange hurts and feels as deeply as anyone else. They are just able to pick themselves up, dust themselves off, and quickly move on with their life. Their great sense of humor is often used to hide a lot of their pain.

On the opposite end of the scale, psychologists at the University of Texas have been studying relationships and the tools for a successful marriage for over ten years. An on-going study has been following 168 couples who have been married since 1981. One of the findings to the success of long-term relationships has certainly shown itself to be the value of a slow and steady courtship. Slow and deliberate most often does win out in the long term over the Hollywood-type romance.

The Rainbow of Relationship Combinations

In between these extremes are the vast majority of others. When two people enter into a relationship, it combines two distinct personalities. Whether they are similar types or quite opposite, some general characteristics will show in their partnerships. The following sections look at each of our various relationship combinations.

Blue and Gold: Do it my way or do it together?

As the road sign says: "Caution, speed bumps ahead!" Blues and Golds view the world through quite different sets of eyes. When this relationship works well, it is a great balance between getting the job done and caring about others. Both have very strong family and relationship values and enjoy lending a hand to help. Golds possess a natural sense of duty, which also applies to their workplace. Overall, Golds prefer to have a smaller group of long-time friends. In fact, others frequently view them as reserved, or business-like, when they first meet. They value their privacy and are quite happy with their small circle of friends. Their strengths and interests lie in getting the job done, along with communication that is straightforward and to the point. This is an area where they start differing from Blues.

The Gold partner often has difficulty understanding or seeing the Blue's deep feelings or motivators in life. Blue has a much stronger relationship drive and always feels the more friends the better. An early challenge in the relationship often comes when Blue invites groups of friends over unannounced. For Golds, their home is their castle and they value privacy. Having larger groups over is not their first choice. It is fine if it's been planned, but somewhat unnerving if it's done as a drop-in basis. The Blue partner is more of a dreamer and quite a bit more creative. It is often difficult for Golds to see their motivations in these areas, or respond to their strong desire for quantity and quality time together, along with frequent hugs and outward signs of affection. That is not the world of Golds who are more comfortable in their task-oriented and practical *today* outlook on life. They value their strengths of being good providers, reliable, and the *reality checker* of the relationship.

As Blues have a difficult time asking straight out for many things, communicating effectively can be an issue in this relationship. It can become a challenge to communicate with Golds in direct ways they understand. For them, conversations do not involve much small talk. Golds get to the point and speak in a straightforward manner. To Blues, they often have to get to the point of anger or crying before they will feel heard or understood. It is also not helpful that Golds do not enjoy being told what to do. They value being the decision-maker and believe they're the best suited for it. Almost every Blue knows they require hugs, reassurance, and to be listened to. The challenge for Golds is to put their agenda aside and just listen. They also need to honor what Blues really value in the relationship. This includes giving in more often, learning that nothing is ever black or white for Blues, and that simple quantity means very little to Blues, who put their heart into everything. Often Blues will fulfill their need to nurture and taking care of others through involvement with charities, or other causes. It becomes a place where Blues receive a large part of their self-esteem in an environment where they are needed and can contribute.

Points of disagreement between these two are in the areas of time management and sticking to a specific plan. These are both big yardsticks for Golds to measure a relationship against, and are large stressors when Blues do not honor their needs in these areas. As high as time management is on the

We've done all the tests, but when she says "Code Blue" she's definitely not referring to a medical condition.

list of Gold priorities, it is not the case for their partner. For Blues, if others need them in any way, the agreed to schedule, plan, or timetable will readily change. For Blues, their friends, family, and coworkers always come first, often at the expense of their own needs or feelings, and certainly as a much bigger priority than any paperwork or task could ever be.

Green and Blue: Think it through or feel it first?

Between these two, the spectrum of living in the heart versus living in the head is certainly covered. While neither needs to be in control or overpowering, the most valuable lesson to learn for the Blues is the need for alone time for their Green partner. Being alone is a stress for Blues who love their interaction with others, while Greens value and seek this time for themselves.

Green time is something few Blues immediately understand or relate to. In addition, a Green partner needing this alone time is often viewed in terms of "what have I done wrong?" or "why is he or she mad at me?" Both enjoy and value the stability of a committed relationship. At the beginning, both may still have lingering difficulties with their previous relationships, however Greens may re-live it in their mind and analyze it from every angle along with their natural inclination to keep beating themselves up over past events. Blues have a very difficult time ending any relationships, as their heart is totally involved in connections with others, which means significant heartache when a relationship is over.

In this team, Blue is always the caregiver, as well as the caretaker and the heart of the relationship. It will be the person that remembers birthdays and anniversaries for both partners, and does the majority of housework, shopping, and little things around the home. Greens really value their Blue partners for this. It takes many things off their plate that seem more important to others. A Green single person will often eat irregularly and can go a long time without buying new clothes, or even giving much thought to housework.

All those great strengths of Blues allow the Green partner to stay focused on the big issues of life and not have to deal with the sometimes tedious or mundane daily needs and tasks. When it comes to things like dinner parties or inviting others over, it is most likely the Blue person who makes any social events happen. They love their time with friends and family and never really understand why their Green partner needs time away from the group after a certain period. They are, however, very proud of the knowledge, intelligence, and calm demeanor of their Green partner. It is a person they can lean on, someone that often has simple solutions and is able to bring problems back to their real size. Communication for these two becomes a more challenging matter. Greens are generally people of few words who prefer conversations that deal with logic and fact and have substance. To them, their Blue partner can sometimes talk too much, while the Blue feels that their partner almost never really does talk or share their feelings.

High Greens can also have the view that their Blue partner is overly emotional, and does not look at many things rationally or logically. It is often a puzzle to them how someone can not only get their feelings easily hurt, but can take some very simple things to heart. That is something the Blue has to teach their Green partner, along with continuously prodding them to expand their conversations and not just relate the facts. They also strengthen the relationship when they teach Greens the real objective in a lot of their conversations. That is, just to be honored by being listened to. Not fixed, no matter how easy or logical the solution appears to their partner. Just to be listened to – and heard.

Orange and Gold: Should we wing it or make a plan?

If opposites do attract, this is certainly one example of such a relationship. This is the blend of the Orange multi-tasker, a flexible and accomplished entrepreneur, combined with the Gold preference for planning and structure. Both combine very different strengths and attitudes in their relationship. When it works, and each person can contribute their strengths to the partnership, it becomes a powerful team.

The Orange contributes greatly through their ideas and creativity along with their endless energy and networking skills. The Gold partner is fine with being the backroom person in

Sure, we have lots in common - like that we're both impatient. I want to get it done and off my list and you want to get it done because you're getting bored with it.

the relationship, letting Orange be the center of attention. They know their contribution to the relationship are their steady and traditional views, organizational strengths, and being the *closer,* or *finisher,* when necessary. With so much on the go, Orange is very grateful to have a high Gold in their life, if they stay supportive and do not interfere and attempt to change the Orange personality. Someone that can take care of the details and stay on track is of great value to them, assuming it does not stymie their high energy or need for freedom. If a Gold starts to exhibit behaviors to control their Orange partner, trouble will soon follow. Golds often shake their head at the ability of the Orange to make so many things turn out successfully with so little apparent planning.

Golds value their Orange partner's hands-on skills, their flexibility, and their ability to work well under stress. They marvel at their *No Fear* and *Just Do It* attitude, consistently positive outlook, and never taking no for an answer. Golds watch their Orange partner try almost anything without a plan and talk to total strangers in any situation, and are often left shaking their heads in amazement.

It can sometimes actually be a little embarrassing for a Gold whose personality generally does not include those traits. Deep down, however, they are very proud of their Orange partner's abilities.

Both know well how to look out for number one, even though it manifests itself in unique ways. Often, an ideal work combination for both is to be self-employed. If they were able to work together on their specific strengths, the Orange would be the marketing, sales, and public face for the business. Vast numbers of Orange are, in fact, self-employed. It gives them the freedom from rules and corporate structure that they want to avoid at all costs. The Gold is the ideal person to handle the other end of the business – the banking, ordering, accounting, personnel, and other behind-the-scenes work. Just like at home, Golds will often marvel at the ability, flexibility, attitude and talents of their Orange partner.

The Gold demeanor tends to be one of a generally concerned outlook. While that is their strength in looking at the practical *what can go wrong* things, it becomes a significant problem if it is something that the Gold wants to *teach* their Orange partner. It is already a challenge to have an argument or fight between these two. Golds prefer to argue in a logical step-by-step manner. One thing at a time, get through it and move on. That is not the style of Oranges. Their main motivation is generally to win. That often extends into fights or arguments. The need to win frequently makes them personalities who do not *fight fair*. They will bring up unrelated issues, and will not want to be locked in to fighting on a point-by-point basis.

The general Gold demeanor of planning and being concerned can also lead to trouble. Gold may be very happy in the relationship, but they are typically not walking through the house whistling or singing. When Oranges are out of esteem, they can tend to take this as "I can't make you happy." The Orange definition of happy always does include being upbeat, outgoing, and whistling or singing. That is not how Golds express their happiness, which is a valuable lesson for Oranges to remember.

Green and Orange: Think before acting or just try it?

This is a relationship that is not dominated by either person. Both are quite independent in their unique ways and often really wonder how the other person functions. For Greens, their partner is almost a mystery to be studied or understood. The Orange partner makes up the outgoing, active, and daring part of the relationship. They shoot from the hip and say what is on their mind. Something like alone time is actually avoided by most Oranges. They look forward to their large circle of buddies and are happiest when they can network and interact with others. Get-togethers, dinner parties, dancing, and almost all other social interactions are great stimuli for Oranges. These times raise their energy level, rather than draining it.

That is quite the opposite for their Green partner. For them, social interactions and get-togethers are much less frequent. A typical Orange party consists of lots of music, high energy, and plenty of action. Greens look for a quieter environment where they can actually hear and be heard, with conversations that are much more focused. Oranges understand quickly that large parts of their social life may well be without their partner. Greens value their *alone-time* and they are people of few words – another large difference. If they allow their Orange partner to push their comfort zones, they will certainly become more balanced in their social interactions. Their Orange partner will pull them out of their shell and involve them in a wide range of social situations.

In return, taking the frequent, and not totally thought-through ideas of the Orange, and filtering them through the mind of the Green partner makes a powerful combination. The creative ideas that come into the Orange mind are run through the *computer* of the Green mind. Greens value their knowledge and ability to research and learn about almost anything. If Oranges have the patience to honor their partner with the time to refine and think through their ideas, they will benefit from some great input and feedback. Greens may have fewer things on the go, but they know it will be more thoroughly researched and well thought out. The Orange partner relies on their friends to network and gather information to make quick

**Don't move, dear. That was a nasty fall.
I'll go e-mail an ambulance for you.**

decisions. Greens instead, prefer to gather material themselves without relying on others. By that time, most Oranges may well have moved on to something else already.

A final sore point between these two can be the issue of what to wear. Oranges love the latest, cool fashions while their Green partner tends to place little value on something so trivial. Just wearing something is often good enough and not subject to spend a great amount of time or thought on. Often, these two do make great friends. In friendships, however, they are able to go their own way at the end of a date. In an actual relationship, Oranges will find just getting the Green to commit may be a significant hurdle. There can be challenges in this long-term relationship. However, with mutual understanding, strong communication tools and a determined effort to value each other's strengths and stresses, it can be a great combination of personalities.

Gold and Green: Take it off the list or make it perfect?

As the heading describes, with these two, it is a relationship focused primarily on task-oriented things. People and their feelings will likely take a back seat to practicality, logic, and getting the job done with this pair. Golds value learning, growing, and being receptive to changes from their Green partner's strengths of finding better solutions and methods. It is someone that will give them a big picture perspective, and who knows that there is more to life than black or white. Seeing possibilities, and getting out of their focus on today, and the job at hand are important lessons for Golds.

In return, Greens will have someone who will ground them and keep them on track in viewing life in realistic terms. Both are very practical people. Greens prefer to see things in terms of the big picture, and appreciate the Gold focus on getting the details and daily stuff done. This ranges from feedback on what to wear to nudging them out of their alone time and toward more social interactions. It is also the practical side of Golds that keeps track of birthdays, sending thank you cards, staying attuned to social rules, shopping and other tasks.

An often seen stress in the relationship revolves around getting something done versus making it right or perfect. Greens will be laid-back, more relaxed, and often passive in the relationship, while Golds are the *on the go* people with definite ideas of what has to be done and when. Something like fixing the computer, the car, the garage door opener, or a renovation project can become a fight between them. To the Gold mindset, once something is started, it needs to be finished. That may make for long days, or even hiring someone, but the prime motivation is to have it off their list. That is not necessarily the view of Greens. Tinkering, experimenting, taking some time to research options, or mulling over some alternatives, can make this a fun and rewarding project for them.

Golds seeing this, immediately realize that none of those adjectives convey the words *finished soon*. In that same vein, it is very helpful when Greens have their own space somewhere in the house that is not shared. The expression "everything in its place" is not one Greens are likely to have much interest in learning – something that can drive their Gold partner nuts. What this partnership does not have a problem with is the Green need for some alone-time each day. Chances are there is always still something to do on the Gold's list and they may not even notice their partner has faded away.

Orange and Blue: Get over it or let the feelings linger?

These two certainly cover the broad *people* spectrum as opposed to their Green and Gold friends. Blues experience people in the ways of intimacy, caring, and through the depth of their emotions and relationships. Oranges experience them through their extensive friendships, high energy, charm, and steadfast optimism. While they certainly enjoy each other's company, these two also have challenges in understanding each other or relating to some of their values. Sometimes they can wonder how the other half lives. For Blues it is a core desire for strong and meaningful relationships; they value intimacy, their home, and the nurturing and caring they share with others. For their partner, the Orange relationships are acceptable if they are more superficial. They love to have a large circle of friends, but in the eyes of their Blue partner, that definition tends to be more of buddies instead of friends. Blues look for close friends that will share from the heart and be active listeners, taking the time to care, share, listen, and understand.

Since Blues have the ability to be intuitive, they know their Orange partner means well and cares about them. Oranges can pull them out of their depression, easily get them to lighten up, and be a great help when Blues needs to be cheered up. Orange is the reality check for the Blue personality. On the other hand, they can also drive them to hurt feelings with their general nature of shooting from the hip with comments or when answering questions. Oranges tend not to be the most patient listeners and will exhibit a selfish streak from time to time. Those are certainly stresses to their Blue partner who views life as a team effort and not a solo performance. They will also get hung up on promises or commitments made by Oranges, or have lasting hurt feelings after an argument, even though it is likely that their Orange partner has forgotten the issue and has long moved on.

Another talent they both share is their ability to multi-task along with putting people ahead of the job. For that reason, both have a tendency to set their watches ahead as a common stress is that they will catch themselves running late. Oranges get sidetracked with too many things on the go, while Blues find it happening when others need them.

Orange can learn from their partner that it is not okay to hurt the feelings of others, especially when it can happen so quickly with their off the cuff comments. When their partner starts to be perceived as needy or clingy however, Orange may start tuning out. They will sometimes admit that when their partner starts being overly emotional or cries too often it becomes a real difficulty for them to deal with. Blues have feelings and commitments that run deep; they look for the good in everyone and will forgive and forgive. They will not easily forget, however. Getting their feelings hurt too often can start compounding and lead to walls coming up to protect themselves. The challenge for Blue in this relationship is not to make their Orange partner feel trapped or confined. When they sense this boxed-in feeling it is possible for them to run or quit on the relationship.

Gold and Gold: Taking care of business

Of all the Color combinations, this is the definitive *getting it done* team. While it would be too strong to state that this focus is at the expense of others, it is certainly fair to say that other people often have to wait until the job is complete. These two will accomplish anything they set their mind to. Both are primarily task-oriented and prefer to plan, execute, and move on. There is not any discussion or wasted time when they are on task. To others, these two do miss some of the subtleties and fun things of life. When they frequently view things in terms of black or white, shades of gray, alternatives, or middle ground is often not seen by this team. This either-or can frequently also be applied to sharing work around the house. Their approach often extends to their preference for the separation of duties in the relationships. Instead of a sharing and pitching in approach, there tends to be a clear division of duties. This type of arrangement allows each to measure when they are done, and esteems them by knowing they have fixed and firm responsibilities that they always need to take care of. It also avoids a conflict of who is the boss and who's to-do list something is on.

Both partners have strong leadership skills and prefer to be the decision-makers in the relationship, which can be a cause of conflict. As neither of them really enjoys being told what to do, or presented with a ready-made decision, this can become an issue. Learning to share both the duties and responsibilities and being open to the wishes of the other are valuable lessons for this Gold team. In fact, one partner will sometimes exhibit one trait that really seems to go against their personality style, something that lets them feel in control in a specific way. This can range from adapting a habit of being late to not finishing certain tasks or projects.

It is very likely that both will be involved with service clubs, their church, community groups, or other charities. Their sense of duty and responsibility makes them strongly value contributing to the world around them with their time and talents. The primary focus on tasks means this team can fail to place emphasis on nurturing each other, or spending time to grow the relationship. Recognizing the value of quality time and building the depth of the relationship are important issues. Both of them will generally have a tight circle of friends whom they treasure, along with their strong bonds with their families. Both are very good with money and savings, and are valued and loyal employees if they work outside the home. They share conservative and traditional values and are comfortable in their knowledge that they can trust each other to always be good to their word and keep their promises.

Their home will be neat and orderly and both are secure in the firmly established, seldom changing routine of their lives. A relationship often starts between two Golds as great friends for extended periods. These two certainly do make ideal friends.

Orange and Orange: The power couple makes it happen

Action and adventure are two appropriate adjectives to describe this couple. Often, Oranges relate the story of how they first met and immediately started dating and becoming involved with each other. Their quick decision-making process often does relate to the manner in which they enter into relationships. The Orange energy, networking, and need to always be on the go – times two! They are certainly a high-energy power couple that everyone else will be hard-pressed to keep up with. They are easy to notice and are a magnet for others because of their humor, action, style, and drive to have fun wherever they are, whatever they are doing. Freedom, creativity, and avoiding boredom at all costs rule the lives of these two. They will be game to try almost anything and live life by their own rules, which are not necessarily those of everyone else.

Yea feels weird. This is our first night at home in 2 weeks. It's not right...we've got to do something tonight...

The Orange energy levels feed off each other, as does their strong sense of competition. After all, winning is everything for Oranges and they are now with a partner that will put up a good fight no matter what the challenge. From sports to work, almost anything can be turned into a competition for them. With their desire for freedom, it is likely that at least one of these two are self-employed. With both partners networking, and with their vast circle of friends, business will be good. While others tend to judge them as workaholic, that is not how the Oranges view it – they are challenged and fulfilled as long as there is action, variety, and freedom in what they do. At the end of the day, there is probably someone with strong organizational skills and attention to detail to actually manage their company. The day-to-day business details are best left for others that value their desk jobs and routines. Those things are not meant to rule the lives of these two, or detract them from really living. After all, if life isn't one big party to live and enjoy – it probably should be. "We're here for a good time, not a long time" is a good saying for them.

Oranges are game to try almost anything, so together they feed off each other's competitive drive and winning attitude. "What can go wrong?", "we can do anything" is frequently what goes through their minds. Neither of them strongly value any time alone and their biggest challenge is to stay with their original commitment and see something through to completion. If one partner values something strongly, that challenge can become a stress in the relationship. With many things on the go, their focus can drift and they often allow themselves to find any excuse to get sidetracked from tasks or duties. The large number of things happening in their lives can also lead them to feel that they are in over their heads in honoring commitments. It is something they will only rarely admit, but it does become an issue in their active lives. With that much happening, both Orange partners can find themselves without a free night for weeks on end. If their commitment or focus tends to be superficial, that can also manifest itself in the bonds of the relationship. The attraction is certainly the common strengths they share, however they are often quite satisfied remaining in a common-law relationship.

Green and Green: The thinking couple

This combination of two Greens tends to be a rare find. Green females constitute a very low percentage of the population, making it difficult for these two to find each other. While it may be an infrequent occurrence, these two have a relaxed and easygoing style in their relationship. Neither of them will bother too much with the details of life, nor get hung up on trivial matters. What to eat, what to wear, when to eat, or remembering to do chores are not priorities to Greens.

As in their interactions with others, they will overlook the annoying behaviors of their partner. After all, the primary focus is on the big picture. Expending negative energy and causing conflict is not the Green style. They will either ignore things, or not even notice. Both love doing their own thing, and relish having a partner that respects their need for space and time alone without pushing or nagging them. Their home will have a fair amount of hi-tech gadgets and probably the latest and greatest computer equipment. Both enjoy reading a great deal, although it is often restricted to non-fiction which allows them to keep learning and growing. Their home will certainly have puzzles, trivia games, or crosswords somewhere nearby. With their thirst for knowledge and their thrill of learning, they love discussions and stimulating conversations with likeminded friends.

They value spirited exchanges with others that can match their intellect, whether they be friends, co-workers, or their partner. If that were not possible in the relationship, it would be a great void in their lives. The shared bond of seeking knowledge and understanding is very strong with these two Greens. Their home will likely be nowhere as organized as that of their Gold friends. Again, this is something that is not a priority to them. There may be a room or garage with electronics equipment, computers, or even cars taken apart and in the process of being fixed. These projects are more like hobbies as opposed to things that need to be done today. It is the thrill of being able to take something apart, understanding how it works or making it better, faster, or more efficient that is at the root of the project. To the outside world, the biggest missing piece in this relationship is the warmth, feeling, and physical touch exhibited by other couples. While Greens feel and care just as deeply, their external demeanor will be more aloof and reserved. With their common traits, these two will often meet as friends and their relationship will develop from there.

Blue and Blue: The feeling and caring couple

Similar to the Green-Green couple, this is another example of an infrequently found relationship. Unfortunately, the percentage of Blue males is as limited as that of Green females. The depth and total commitment to each other show very clearly in this Blue-Blue team. A double Blue relationship means a total focus on each other, a strong bond, and shared values.

When these two people are committed to each other, it creates a formidable bond. To friends and others, this shows in many ways. It is one of the relationship combinations that tends survive the test of time. As both partners are very attuned to each other's feelings and emotions, it is rare that significant problems arise. Building a strong and lasting relationship comes without effort for either of these two. It is part of their personality to always look out for others. That shows in their caring and warmth at work, as well as their drive to help others less fortunate through charities or church groups. With this motivation, and a large part of building their self-esteem, it goes without saying that this same care and compassion starts at home with each other. To the Blues, life is all about the relationship and shared feelings.

Their difficulty in asking for anything for themselves and willingness to bend to the plans and wishes of others make them a comfortable fit. It means they are both very unselfish and respectful to the wishes of each other. It is only when they are out of esteem that they exhibit any selfishness, yelling, or acting out behaviors. They connect with each other through their hearts, and their great intuitive abilities allow them to stay aware of the state of their partner.

There is seldom any fighting with these two. Neither partner requires or values control, or finds any need for power struggles. To them, relationships are all about sharing, caring, and listening. They are about dreaming and growing together as a team and sharing their journey together. Both make each other their first priority and know they will always have a safe haven from the world when they are together. It is not getting the job done that is their primary focus, but rather the opportunity to do it together. They share a large circle of friends whom they treasure and love spending time with. Both, of course, are great listeners and are always there as a shoulder to cry on.

Blues are excellent multi-taskers that like to do a quality job. What is missing is any strong drive to complete the task or the Green trait to think it through versus feeling everything in the heart. But as the saying goes: "You don't miss what you don't have," which can well apply to this pair.

A final thought comes from the Saskatoon Pastoral Institute Newsletter. It outlines ten steps for NEVER having an intimate relationship. Sad, but true, each Color is amply represented:

1. Don't talk – if you are forced to talk stick to small-talk and avoid discussing true feelings.

2. Never show your feelings – showing any emotions gives you away, thus they must be avoided.

3. Always be pleasant – especially if something's wrong – it's important to fool your partner.

4. Always win – don't compromise or it becomes a dangerous precedent to showing you care.

5. Always keep busy – it allows you to hide and send the clear message that work is more important than your relationship.

6. Always be right – among other things, it allows you to keep the upper hand and stay in control.

7. Never argue – or you might discover you are different, which would mean making allowances, adjustments, and compromises. THAT could lead to letting your partner see who you really are or know what you really feel.

8. Make your partner guess what you want – when they guess wrong, which they will often, you are able to tell them they really don't understand or love you.

9. Always look out for number one – after all, you are the one making all the sacrifices in the relationship.

10. Keep the TV on at all times – especially if you're talking. Best of all, nobody will even notice that you don't communicate.

Chapter 9

Colors at Work

For most of us, work consumes a large part of our life. If opposites attract in relationships, that is definitely not the case in the workplace. Yet this is an area where we interact with dozens, often hundreds of people we didn't even get to choose ourselves. Turnovers, transfers, promotions, department mergers, and a host of other events cause us to be thrown together with people we don't know and didn't pick, and with whom we have to spend a significant part of our day.

Sometimes staff are quite convinced that employees who are not like them are a punishment sent from the Human Resources Department. Surely they'll come around soon enough, or maybe they just lie awake at night thinking of ways to annoy others? How many people would save countless aggravations and stresses if they understood their teams' Colors and the unique strengths each person contributes? How many bosses would reduce their turnover if they simply used the basic lessons of personality types?

> *"You'll never (really) get people to work for you,*
> *but you can get people to work with you."*
> Murray Koffler, Founder: Shoppers Drug Mart

It can sometimes seem that we are waiting for others to come around, for them to be just like the rest of the staff and *fit in* or adapt. Well, it is not likely to happen. In the workplace, the wide varieties of personalities are like the various pieces of a jigsaw puzzle. Each person has different communication methods, values, general demeanors, and most certainly a wide range of approaches to life at work. For every company and team, most of the conflicts in relating to others can be easily improved by recognizing, understanding, and valuing this diversity.

**I have a meeting with my boss tonight,
so I just need to have one drink.**

Different strokes for different folks – but that is something everyone knows already and it is not enough is it? The strengths, stresses, and diversity of the four types never shows more clearly than at work. Just like the spokes in a wheel, each of the unique personality styles is needed for a well functioning company. Just as everyone strives for balance in their own life, so a company looks for that same balance in their workforce. After all, finding, hiring, and training staff is a very expensive proposition. Most companies accomplish this through hiring and promoting staff with a variety of traits, experiences, and strengths into specific positions. Often this happens through trial and error as employers find their *perfect* employee and those same employees search for their ideal job.

> *"Coming together is a beginning.*
> *Keeping together is progress.*
> *Working together is success."*
> Henry Ford

No matter what anyone's job description says, the main challenge for any firm is to have their staff work in harmony. To have teams working together toward common goals, with everyone contributing in their own ways to achieve that end. As if operating a company is not intricate enough, on top of that is added the balancing of various needs, personality styles, job descriptions, politics, and other intangibles involved in managing staff. Different Colors look for different values and motivators in the workplace. The firm's attitude toward teamwork, the manner of cooperation, socializing, management styles, and the ways employees are treated play a large factor for different Colors.

One of the best examples of attracting and balancing Colors in the workplace is that of Primerica Financial Services. With more than 110,000 representatives across North America, this is a company which understands diversity. As a subsidiary of Citigroup, and with over six million clients, it attracts vast numbers of representatives of all Colors, but appeals to each of them for very different reasons.

Part of Primerica's mission statement is to be in the business of changing lives. They most certainly do – for clients, as well as for their teams. As a company rapidly growing in numbers and expanding internationally, their appeal reaches across all Color groups. Small wonder it is a firm that continues to be one of the leaders in the field of sales training, standing head and shoulders above almost any other financial services company.

First and foremost is their unique approach to hiring. It starts with the presumption that everyone has the tools to become successful, in their unique way, and on their own terms. It is not a system that pre-judges, assumes, or screens out applicants that may not *fit* after a 15 minute interview. Is that really the place to judge someone's long-term success? Primerica understands that pre-screening eliminates vast numbers of applicants that will become very successful with the company. For many firms it is generally our Orange friends that will not make it past the initial interviews. Yet this is the group who are the most successful sales and marketing people anywhere.

What attracts individuals to a first career night, what we value, and how we sell are very much inter-related as any Primerica representative will tell you. After all, we are always sold on anything in our very unique *language*. In the same manner, we use this language when we communicate, listen, or buy, whether that is a product, service, or ourselves.

For Golds it is the strength, stability, and reputation of the company – being #1 on the Forbes Super 500 and well established since 1977. For Blues it is the unwavering commitment to building long lasting relationships. Greens are attracted because of the leadership, future visions of the company, and ability to structure a large part of their work in their own fashion and on their own terms.

Finally, of course, the largest group of representatives are the Oranges. For them, it is the opportunity to have freedom from too much control, and to work for a company that places significant emphasis on practicality, fun, high energy, and a positive environment. The chance to be paid based on what they achieve, along with significant numbers of contests, awards, and an environment free of routines also acts as a huge magnet to the Oranges.

Work Questions to Ask

Whether out loud or not, there are some basic questions each group tends to ask themselves about any job or company:

Golds

- Will you trust me to do the job, let me control my agenda, and not ride me?

- Am I going to have a sense of belonging here?

- Do you recognize staff for their contributions in fair and tangible ways?

- Will I have clear and consistent instructions, expectations, rules, and time-lines?

Golds want their workplace to be organized and scheduled with routines and fixed procedures. They look for others to stick to the facts and follow an agenda, staying on track and making decisions that are not subject to significant changes, vagueness, or variables.

Blues

- Does the company listen to me and my needs?

- Will I have assistance for conflict and problem solving?

- Is the boss someone who listens well and respects my feelings and those of others?

- Do I get to use my people skills with clients and staff, or is the day all task-oriented?

Blues work best in a creative and positive environment which allows them personal freedom without too many rules, fixed procedures or routines. They look for companies that foster an atmosphere where everyone is included and heard.

Greens

- Am I allowed sufficient independent work time?

- How much of the position is re-active or pro-active?

- Are procedures logical or are they bogged down with *stupid* rules and set in stone?

- Can I help teach others and keep learning, growing, and asking questions?

Greens need efficiencies in procedures much more than traditions or defined routines and boundaries. They have very high standards, and often show a single-minded determination to reach their goals.

Oranges

Do I know *what's in it for me*?

Are there enough new challenges, problems to solve, and is there variety every day?

Is it a fun environment? Can I move around? How hung up are you on rules and fixed procedures?

If I can handle six things at once, is there teamwork to help me finish the details and paperwork?

Oranges work at their best when they are able to fix problems hands-on, while paying less attention to the details, policies, or routine paperwork.

Who Are We at Work?

Individuals always have a choice of where they work, and in what type of job. Few however, have the option of choosing their fellow employees.

Two of the keys to working as an actual team are awareness and acceptance. Awareness starts with understanding everyone's differences, unique characteristics, values, and motivations. Also important is understanding their sense of humor, ways of learning, how they contribute to the team, and how individual styles get their jobs done.

Here are some basic strengths that both employees and managers contribute to the workplace through their unique Colors.

Blue Employees

- Prefer sensing and feeling the caring, teamwork, and support from others

- Value honesty and caring with constructive suggestions and feedback

- Look for bosses that value them, listen well, and respect their feelings

- Look for unstructured and informal meetings which encourage shared feelings and participation

- Feel uncomfortable and stressful when conflict arises

Blue Managers

- Enjoy real relationships and interactions with employees

- Develop an open and democratic workplace environment

- Receive great self-satisfaction when employees grow

- Manage through encouraging and supporting others as unique individuals

- Welcome and promote input from their team into decision making

Blue Team Members

- Mediators, people oriented, and peace-makers

- Prefer cooperation to competition

- Intuitive, imaginative, and always caring for others and their feelings

- Easily feel and share the pain of others

- Animated expressions – verbalizing their dreams and ideas

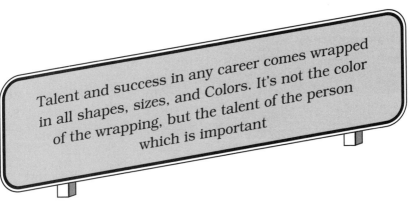

Talent and success in any career comes wrapped in all shapes, sizes, and Colors. It's not the color of the wrapping, but the talent of the person which is important

Orange Employees

- Perform well in any competitive, high action environment

- Look for fun and excitement, not boring routines or structure

- Learn by doing – not by talking

- Like tools, hands-on tasks, and are very creative

- Value flexibility and new ideas over fixed written outlines

Orange Managers

- Give employees goals and feedback that are immediate and concrete

- Excellent lateral-thinker and practical problem solver

- Prefer direct results working hands-on versus theoretical methods

- Encourage an exciting, high energy, and creative workplace
- Fun and flexible leadership approach without too much emphasis on details or micro-management

Orange Team Members

- Self-confident, highly energetic, and easy to get along with
- Open minded, very flexible, and quick decision-maker
- Love tools and creativity – the latest, greatest stuff
- Competitive – tests rules, limits and boundaries, great risk taker
- Multi-taskers, entertainers, and excellent negotiators

Gold Employees

- Perform best when jobs are planned and scheduled
- Value feedback to know they're doing the right thing
- Seek clearly outlined directions, rules, and guidelines
- Trust them to get the job done when promised without the need for extensive follow-up
- Stick to the facts, want the details, get to the point, and make a decision

Gold Managers

- Work areas are well organized and procedures are established and followed
- Discipline in a consistent and fair manner
- Value, support, and lead team efforts
- Develop upgrading and learning in a *one thing at a time* manner
- Value training and growth for employees and acknowledge them as the foundation of an organization

Gold Team Members

- Dependable, task oriented, providing sense of security
- On-time, well planned out and prepared
- Perform in structured, detailed, and consistent manner

- Helpful and supportive to team and management
- Loyal, traditional, and maintains status quo
- Place great importance on company reputation

Green Employees

- Perform best when seeing the big picture and overall logic
- Value and seek their time to work independently
- Challenged by interpreting fresh suggestions and probing abstract ideas and plans
- Logical, theoretical, and good grasp for the intangible
- Value feedback that recognizes their competence and knowledge

Green Managers

- Management strengths through growing the competency of other staff
- Gets satisfaction from developing new systems to reflect technological advances
- Excel in teaching others through their own continuous learning and research
- Challenges others to make it perfect and think it through
- Approach problems and solutions in a logical manner

Green Team Members

- Big picture visionary always looking for improved methods
- Evaluate all possibilities before making a decision
- Practical decision-makers in a democratic environment
- Intellectual and creative problem solvers - exploring all possibilities
- Love technology, learning, and discovering
- Always inquisitive

*"When working together, average people
can accomplish incredible things. Together they'll
accomplish things a little better, a little faster,
and always toward excellence."*

Acceptance is definitely the harder part of the equation. People tend to get their back up over differences in others. Everyone is quite sure that others would fit in better if they just worked *like me.* Colors, time and again, is one of the best methods and tools to achieve understanding and teamwork. It is the personality differences that create stress and confrontation. Teamwork and unity come about when there is genuine appreciation for diversity. It is the understanding of these differences that makes any group work well together. Some team members contribute great strengths in dealing with customers, while others deal well with problems and managing a crisis. Others are very detail-oriented or can better see the big picture. Yet another group contributes in large ways through their great sense of humor, high energy, and constant can-do attitude.

The two largest groups of self-employed entrepreneurs are Gold and Orange. Gold will generally purchase existing businesses with a proven track record. Oranges are much more of the risk-takers, jumping into new businesses that feel right, promise a lot of action, and use their strengths in marketing, people skills, networking and creativity.

The more diversity there is in any team, the more effective, powerful, and productive it becomes. By standing together, teams, departments, and entire companies are strong. Individual employees, no matter how talented, are no match for any competition. It takes an entire team effort to be successful and have everyone pulling in the same direction. That does not mean everyone has to share the same values or outlook. Different opinions, just like having different job functions, is not a detriment to the team, but rather quite an asset.

After all, would a perfect football team consist of nothing but quarterbacks? Or would anyone really bet on the five highest scoring forwards in hockey winning many games together? Of course the answer to these is no. Any sports team requires specialists in various positions, with different strengths. When these individual stars are combined with others and their talents, it creates powerful teams. The key is the balance of talents and strengths. This holds true for companies, just as it does for individuals.

"You're gonna see a guy who will sacrifice himself for this team. Because when it comes down to it, you're gonna do the same for him. That's a team, gentlemen – and either we heal now as a team, or we will die as individuals. Now what are you going to do?"
Al Pacino: Any Given Sunday

High Blues can be really poor salespeople if forced to market something they don't believe in. If they do believe in the product or service, they are almost unstoppable and wildly successful, building strong relationships in ways others can only dream about.

It's not Always about Money

Employers need to foster an environment where they really care about their staff. In return, staff will actually care about their clients, profitability, and the growth of the company they work for. Meeting those challenges and doing it well pays off through productivity growth, increased profits, reducing turnover, and satisfied repeat customers.

Everyone is familiar with the stories of the companies that do this well. Featured stories of the best Companies to work for is mainly restricted to large National Organizations. However, this leaves out many excellent small and medium sized firms. In that category is Paull Travel in Edmonton, Alberta. Owner Lesley Paull is one of the best examples of living the understanding and use of Colors and team building.

Paull is a strong Orange personality and owner of her own firm. What could be more perfect than a career which allows frequent travel, a wide variety of tasks, and constant interactions with others. All this in an industry fraught with constant challenges and changes. She uses her knowledge to create teams around their personality strengths and selling abilities. Paull set out to match her job descriptions to the Colors of her staff. "I even had some staff that just were not totally comfortable with selling. So I realigned my staff to make that possible."

Today, her staff actually consists of half travel agents, half support staff – something unheard of in the industry, and thought unsustainable by almost all her peers. Good thing Oranges do not make decisions based on the tried and tested methods, or traditional organizational structures.

Radical as it may be, her agency has continued to enjoy unparalleled growth through some of the most difficult and challenging times in the industry. Her Orange staff can excel at their strengths without the stress of excessive paperwork. Her Gold staff do contribute to travel sales, but focus on being teamed up with Orange agents handling the details, planning and paperwork. In fact, Paull has a number of agents whose individual monthly volume exceeds that of an average travel agency. At the end of the day, results speak louder than words, truly a great motto for any Orange.

Paull's definition of support staff, however, is not a typical one. All incentives, bonuses, training, gifts, and trips always encompass her entire team, regardless of job description or title. "We always do everything together. We don't have two different classes of staff – ever," says Paull. In fact, bonuses can sometimes be a significant part of the support staff pay. "I don't judge people on just one scale. Whether they're support or selling agents, they're all equally important."

Even full travel agents utilize different skill sets. Corporate sales are significantly more organized and straightforward. In turn, leisure travel involves much more creativity and time in its planning. Both are major differences Paull is very aware of. Her office functions efficiently and as a team. Business is great, stress is at a minimum, and job functions are geared to utilize everyone's natural talents. How much turnover would she have without using these tools? While she modestly deflects the question, the answer is clear.

Paull relates a typical story that many Oranges love to hear, and are well familiar with. One of her larger clients had changed travel agents for a minor discount with a competitor. It wasn't long before he chose to return, sharing that "they didn't know who I was and never made me laugh." Powerful words frequently heard by Oranges with their high-energy, great enthusiasm, and constant personal touch and attention. This is clearly one of the keys to the continued growth of her business, which is frequently unknown, overlooked or underrated by others.

"The strength of the team is each individual member...
the strength of each member is the team"
Coach Phil Jackson

The Perfect Workplace

In an ideal workplace or office, every Color looks for particular things that they value. Anyone's dream workplace is probably different from someone else's idea. While not many employees can create these perfect environments, here are some general things each Color looks for:

Judging by the look on your faces you're not that keen on changing some of the things we decided last week, are you?

A Great Gold Workplace

"My ideal workplace is well laid out and organized, with clear rules and expectations that are enforced fairly for everyone. I enjoy having my own space and the chance to put up my awards and certificates. I look for superiors that recognize my ability to complete any assignment without follow-up or excuses, and who reward my work regularly and fairly. I value consistent operating standards with fixed and predictable routines and procedures with very little stress or conflict. I look for workplaces that respect my scheduling ability and allow me to work on things that need to be done today, one thing at a time, and without constant interruptions or last-minute changes."

A Great Green Workplace

"My ideal workplace is a wide-open but a low noise area. I look for the chance to have quiet periods of thinking time without interruption or distractions. I want to emulate the structure used by teams of researchers, where there is extensive interaction with others that share my creativity, logic, and strengths of creativity. I love opportunities to discuss and debate complex problems, to have a chance to share my knowledge and research. I seek a boss that is not pushy or in need of instant answers to complex questions. I look for someone who recognizes my strengths of research and innovation, of contributing to the big picture of the department."

A Great Orange Workplace

"My idea of a great workplace has very little structure, rules, or routines. I look for freedom and the chance to get hands-on involvement to make things happen with my creativity and my need for action. I look for a boss that appreciates my high energy, multi-tasking skills, and problem-solving strengths. My company should reward me in real and tangible ways and give me direct and straightforward instructions without too much detail. I love to be let loose on any challenge and work well under stress if I am given the freedom to do my thing."

As employees, Oranges will start looking for another position if their job is perceived as becoming more restrictive with too many rules, or when they feel their fun and freedom are gone.

A Great Blue Workplace

"My ideal workplace promotes and encourages teamwork and open interaction with others. I seek a chance to be involved in the decision-making and the opportunity to verbalize ideas with my team. I treat others as members of my extended family, not just fellow employees. I love working with people that have strong listening skills, respect my opinions, and take me seriously. I am awesome at getting everyone involved and making them feel included. I look for fellow staff that share my strength of verbal communication, and a company that is sensitive to the effect of corporate change on their staff. I look for a workplace that values my contributions in terms of customer service and teamwork, and not only in terms of quantity of work."

I know you feel everybody should be included and heard, Larson - but that could take weeks!

Team Building Pays

In the coming years, companies will continue to move more and more toward an increased emphasis on teamwork. But frequently it is talk and not action. For large numbers of firms, compensation is still not geared toward what is being preached. Promotions or bonuses still go mostly to the superstar solo players. Numerous studies have shown that structuring departments into teams leads to an increase in productivity, and in a measurable improvement of employee retention. The combination of those two results in increased profits and decreased costs in terms of hiring and training expenses.

Talk the Talk but also Walk the Walk

Just paying lip service to the concept of teamwork will not make it happen. Employees have been well taught to notice the *plan of the month*. Policy changes, and new procedures or slogans, frequently come and go. Most employees have *learned* that ignoring these for a certain period of time will, in all likelihood, make them *go away* when the focus of management moves onto different issues. This alone is a real stress for Golds. As this is generally the largest group of employees, changes that come and go but are not enforced can be a significant irritant for them.

Team building and personality type seminars frequently show that when staff are sought out for input, suggestions, and the development of teamwork strategies, they first see this could well be a strategy that is here to stay. It is also apparent that employees who provide input into the development of a wide range of strategies will quite readily buy-in to those same changes, regardless of their primary Color. Besides, anything they have contributed to is difficult to assassinate, since it came from their own ranks.

> Strange but true that the average company spends less than 2% of their training budget on front-line staff. Yet they are the employees that almost single-handedly control customer satisfaction, repeat business, and cross-marketing.

Find the Job You Love

"Do what you love to do and you'll never have to work again!"

Does an individual's personality have an effect on their job and career choices? Can we each really do any job we want? The answer to both is yes – but...

Studies show that the average person will make four or five different career choices throughout their working life. Hopefully, each of them will bring them closer to their dream job, one that not only pays well (the reality of life) but more importantly fits their preferences, ideal work environment, as well as their Colors. Yes, any person can do any job. However, if the personality does not fit the job, it often becomes a question of how long will someone last.

It is proven over and over again that it is impossible to fit any personality type into a specific set of jobs. Most people are very happy in their chosen careers, some experience real challenges, while others are still looking for the knowledge and tools to lead them to their perfect job. A few have even been known to quit after learning about their Colors. Not because of the session, but as the final straw that finally put into words what they have been feeling all along.

For most people, it is the big picture that appeals to them, not any pigeonholed job description matched to any specific Color. It is in the job description, the work environment, the larger corporate culture, and how the position interacts with others that makes it the right fit for them. Different personality types are better suited for certain tasks. When the quantity of these tasks is added up, an entire job description may be much better suited to some groups. Can a Blue person be a really good file clerk? You bet! Will they last for any length of time in a position that has no interaction with others? Not likely. Can an Orange person perform in a strict desk job with constant deadlines, and unwavering rules and procedures? Of course! Will they still be in the position in a year? Don't bet on it.

Lori is a finance manager for a car dealership. She is a Gold/Green (with last color Orange) and works for an even higher Gold boss. Many of the sales staff and other managers are high Orange (the nature of the automotive business), and her job description necessitates spending almost all day in an Orange environment. This means significant and continuous multi-tasking, constant interruptions, people *dropping in* with a lot of traffic in and out of her office, and a need to be totally flexible in any sales approach. Lori has at least 15-20 customers to work with at any one time, and the entire day is spent reacting without being pro-active.

Of course, Lori has not missed many days of work in a decade and can always be counted on to help other staff, cover for them, and go the extra mile without being asked. Her income is almost six figures – who wouldn't want that pay? But the job is quickly burning Lori out and wearing her down. She is a primary Gold caught up in a catch-22 situation. Her Gold wants to retain the great pay, while her very Gold boss allows Lori a fair degree of freedom on most days and or micro-manages on others. She also really hates change of any kind, especially when it comes to switching jobs. However, at the same time she longs to work in a more structured environment, in a job where she can be pro-active, plan, and function with proper schedules and agendas. She craves an environment where she is recognized and valued in ways that cannot simply be measured by looking at her commission check.

Any person can excel at any job. After all, talents truly do come in all Colors. It just takes a significantly higher amount of dedication, concentration, and discipline when a job just isn't *a match* for someone. It sometimes is the equivalent of swimming upstream each and every day. It can be done, but takes significantly more energy and effort than performing at a job and in a work environment that more closely matches someone's personality. People truly can do almost anything they put their mind to when it comes to a choice of jobs, but will it make them happy? Will it create a sense of self-satisfaction or build their self-esteem?

Almost any job requires the use of all four Colors to some degree. We need to have time to have some fun, interact with others, think things through, and be task focused while staying on track. What matters to most people is where the majority of their job description falls. Armed with that understanding, it often becomes a matter of matching the personality of the employee with the Colors required of the job.

"We make our living by what we do
and our life by who we are"

Chapter 10

Kids in Action – Family Dynamics

"I wish that I knew what I know now – when I was younger."
Rod Stewart

Any look at relationships would not be complete without considering those involving kids. From the state of their room, to learning styles and different communication methods, kids show their personality types at a very early age.

In fact, kids are some of the biggest fans of learning these basic tools. Often, within 10 minutes of hearing about it, they are able to put words with behaviors of family members, teachers, and their friends. It gives kids a user-friendly way to express themselves. It allows them to put words to their feelings and emotions, and develops an understanding of their joys and stresses in terms they can easily relate to. Kids everywhere love to test the limits of many things. This is not necessarily an Orange behavior, but one shared by kids everywhere growing up. At the same time as they seek ways to be individuals, they also have a strong need to belong. It is one of the key motivators for kids of all ages.

"I treat all my kids the same" may not be the best approach once you have an understanding of the differences in their personality, needs, and motivators through knowing each of their own unique combination of Colors.

Understanding Colors creates a framework within which kids discover that it is okay to be unique and different from others around them. Peer pressure, school, different parenting styles, and a range of teachers and friends with varying priorities make today's world a difficult minefield to maneuver for kids and teenagers. Colors allows them to better relate to some family members and gives them a greater insight and appreciation of the high Gold school structure.

Remember when I said we should make the living room more fun? When you were leaving you said 'whatever?' Well I took that as a yes!

The basic needs and wants for kids are the same as those of their parents. Kids need to know their parents are 100 percent there for them when they have time together. Just as adults relate to others at work, kids need and deserve that same undivided attention at home. When you're home, are you really there? Are you engaged? Are you mentally, spiritually, and physically there for them? Just as communication styles are different between adults, they are also different for kids' personalities. It needs to be adapted into the *language* of the child, to their Color, and not to the communication preference of the adult or parent.

Imposing rules without having a relationship always causes rebellion. In the same way, talking to kids without knowing their language can create distance and foster the feeling of a real generation gap. Being attuned to their personality becomes a great tool for growing and strengthening the relationship. It also acts as a significant building block for their self-esteem. It's not a job – it's a way of life. The methods however can vary widely amongst parents. For one, it might be a half-hour of quality time spent having breakfast together. In turn, the other parent may feel very badly and apologize to their child that their partner only had that half-hour. Yet for the child it may well have been an awesome time together. The parent wasn't reading the newspaper or on the telephone, instead they had quality child-parent time.

Caution! "It's not fair" is an often-heard saying from kids of all Colors. While this is a very important value for Gold, when kids use the expression it can have vastly different meanings. These interpretations can range from "I want to get my way" to actual Gold fairness issues or a Blue stress of not including everyone.

These are definitely two different views of the same scenario. Was it just breakfast together, or great quality time? Perhaps for the Green child, that means very little conversation, or for the Blue child it may be a long narrative involving their dreams, feelings, or sharing of stories involving their friends. No matter what their Color, the main challenge is to interact with them in a consistent manner on their terms and in their *language*. Children have to know and feel that the parent will have this consistency in their communication style every day, and all the time. After all, for kids it is never the size of the paycheck or the big problems of the work-world, it's all the little things that impact their lives in such powerful and lasting ways too numerous to measure.

High Green Kids

These kids at an early age already value their *Green time* of being alone, reading, doing puzzles, figuring things out on their own, or generally being quite content to entertain themselves. They don't always seek out social situations, and are perfectly comfortable in their own company. These kids can ask a lot of questions in their life-long quest for knowledge, understanding, and growth with their focus on visions and ideas. In the school environment, they typically do not feel that comfortable with many kids, lots of noise, and little time to process or absorb material. Things like team sports and small talk do not appeal to their interests. In later years, the same can be said about dating, social functions, or school dances. They may participate in some of them, but it is not their preferred setting. They value teaching styles that involve logical and well-planned presentation, and consistent opportunities to participate in discussion and debates with the opportunity to ask lots of questions. They enjoy personally researching material and thrive on sharing what they've learned with others. Among their favorite subjects are math, history and science, and any areas involving complex problems or situations which stimulate their minds.

High Orange Kids

Orange kids can be a handful for their parents. Trying anything, naturally curious, pushing boundaries and bending the rules, they are having fun and enjoying the social part of life. They become friends with almost everyone they meet, shoot from the hip, hate losing, and probably have a room that looks like it has been hit by a tornado. The greatest appeal for Orange kids is the stimulation of interacting with others – any social scene. They do not react well to real or perceived boredom and will do whatever is necessary to create a little excitement – not always in positive ways.

They love to perform and be the center of attention, which greatly builds their self-esteem. They are natural leaders in their circle of friends. Others often gravitate to them as the center of activity and they are, for the most part, strong extroverts. The structure, routine, and rules of the school system have very little appeal to Orange kids. They are often judged as underachievers or simply labeled as the class clowns for their behavior in and out of class. Their favorite parts of school are any social settings, including recess, dances, music, and drama where they can perform and learn *practical* things as they judge it. These are also areas that allow them to show off their creative skills and talents through the use of tools or acting.

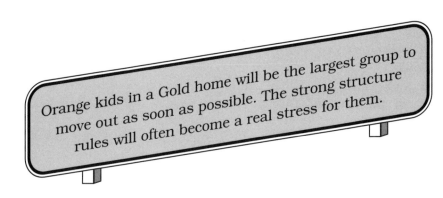

Orange kids in a Gold home will be the largest group to move out as soon as possible. The strong structure rules will often become a real stress for them.

This group learns best when they have hands-on activities and when learning becomes a competition where they have the opportunity to become the *winner*. Orange kids look for practical instructions without a lot of details or rules and flexible, varied, and high energy teaching styles. They seek instant feedback and instructors that are fun, flexible, and innovative. These will not be the kids that will routinely have their assignments done. Written homework is a challenge, since it does not allow them to perform, or use their talent of winging it. It means homework assignments will often not be indicative of their knowledge or understanding of a subject, as it is not a form of communication they favor.

High Blue Kids

Blue kids are emotional and highly sensitive. They already exhibit signs of wearing their heart on their sleeve and can get their feelings hurt easily. They value helping others, which often means bending to the wishes of those around them. They already do their best to be the peacemakers or to smooth things over whenever possible. Because of their good-hearted nature, gift of listening and involving others, they make friends easily. Even as kids, Blues tend to communicate in an animated manner and look for positive reinforcement. They value the physical touch or hugs, and need others to really listen to them and their dreams. The Blue child looks for a group environment and cooperative learning situations where lessons are adaptable to individual needs. They are not interested too much in the process or procedures, but far more in the other kids around them. Stories, interactive games, and any sensory-oriented activities are the easiest ways for them to learn. In school, they tend to love classes involving social studies, music, drama, and any projects they can complete as a team. Recess is also one of their favorite times as it is the chance to interact and visit with their friends.

I'm Blue, so if it's a sad movie I won't be able to invite my friends over. They'll just pick on me when my feelings leak out.

High Gold Kids

This group of kids already have a good sense of responsibility and knowledge of right from wrong at an early age. They are quite comfortable in the background and behind the scenes, instead of being the center of attention. At home they look for stability, fixed routines, and discipline that is perceived to be fair and consistent. They gain self-esteem by contributing and being helpful to others. A small circle of friends is just fine for most Golds, to whom they are very loyal. They will obey rules and follow clear instructions. This also makes them the teacher's pet in school where they are disciplined, pay attention, and do their homework.

They thrive on teaching styles that involve detailed instructions and lesson plans that follow a logical outline, and they value a lot of handouts and resource materials. Among their favorite subjects are band and language arts classes, along with subjects that have right or wrong answers such as math.

Most high Gold kids will likely only skip school a few times in their life. The overriding guilt of getting caught, and knowing they're breaking the rules, really does not make it worthwhile.

At the end of the day, it is always important to remember a wonderful billboard in Chicago: "Don't forget the people you are working for are waiting for you at home." Or Dr. Laura Schlessinger's challenge at the end of her radio talk show: "Now go do the right thing."

Chapter 11

Learning Styles

"Learning that does not increase daily - will daily decrease"
Chinese Proverb

The methods in which individuals learn are very much related to their strengths, stresses, and motivators. In other words, it is also related to their primary Color. The challenge for any instructor or teacher is to first understand the learning preferences of their group. It's important to know your facts, but also to know who you're facing as well. Great instructors and facilitators understand that learning is very much like communication. It is not so much what an instructor is saying, but mainly in what the students are hearing. Added to that is the environment, class layout, speed of covering materials, and how much group participation to include. A vast challenge, indeed, is to accommodate the differences in personalities. Many of the ways people learn, or learn best, relate directly to their motivators and strengths in their Colors.

Different classes lend themselves to different teaching methods. Whether they are school subjects, night classes, or workplace seminars, each setting readily makes for different styles. Sports, classes on welding, carpentry or automotive are much more the environment of Oranges. Drama, music, bible study, self-improvement seminars, creative writing, or social studies classes are some examples that easily allow Blues to shine. Right or wrong answers and structure are generally found in math, cooking, learning a musical instrument or a foreign language. These are settings that Golds value. Greens often enjoy subjects such as science, history or physics, courses which include elements of lectures, group discussions, and the chance to formulate their own reports or input.

The majority of feedback on effective and targeted learning styles comes from teachers and facilitators. What better groups to offer suggestions in this area than with their vast experience in dealing with all personalities. Even before discovering the power of Colors, teachers and facilitators have learned to target their instructions to various groups of personalities for maximum effectiveness. In schools, homes, or workplace training, whether children or adults, learning in today's society is becoming a life-long journey. For each Color to understand their preferences and stresses, and for instructors and teachers to be attuned to the basic differences in learning styles becomes a powerful tool for any instructional environment.

"Learning is what most adults will do for a
living in the 21st Century"
Perelman

The Green Preferences

Greens are generally amongst the quieter and intelligent group of students. Whether in a work seminar or the school system, Greens focus on their studies without much emphasis on the extra curricular matters. As they are frequently people of few words, they will not be vocal, highly active, or the first to participate in discussions. A primary focus for them is the credibility of their instructor. They look for assurances that the person teaching them has a broad knowledge and an in-depth understanding of the material. They value someone that is able to take the specific material at hand and relate it into the big picture. For Greens, two of the more important things in their learning environment are processing time and quiet areas.

Greens seek to fully understand the basics, concept, principles, and specifics of the subject at hand. This ranges from simply having the time to digest and grasp the content of group discussions to dissect the subject matter in detail. To best accomplish this, they look for quiet time. They value processing information on their own time to think things through. This means finding opportunities to get away from the noise of the classroom. The chance to wander off alone during breaks, into the library, or a quieter area of the room allows them to process the material and think it through more thoroughly.

Greens love debates and discussions. They will always admit there aren't many questions they don't want to ponder. Often, the more intricate, the better. Similar to workgroups of scientists or researchers, they thrive on this format of learning and growing. They can certainly play devils advocate just to keep the discussion going, or to pull out all points of view. When these discussions happen in groups of others who they find credible and worthy of challenging them, Greens are very much in their element.

Greens Value

- Learning as a hobby and not a task or chore
- Group brainstorming, but individual reports or assignments
- Many paths to the goal with milestones and deadlines
- Real world problems
- Visual learning
- Clear, simple, and logical instructions related once
- Sufficient research time
- Abstract sequential – need to know the big picture
- Built-in time for questioning and exploration of subject
- Link to future benefit and implications
- Tie-in (fit) of material to what they already know
- Credibility in material and instructor
- Reward for their research, skills, and interpretations
- Lots of available resources, including computers
- High expectations of themselves and instructors
- Time to process, research, mull, discuss, perfect
- Hands-on, living the experience
- A factual and logical focus
- Ability to contribute input, interpretation, and their ideas
- That best efforts are always given and required
- Emphasis on outcomes, results, and implications
- Juicy questions and stimulating discussions

The Orange Preferences

As learning styles are quite different for Oranges, the standard instruction formats can be difficult for them. In any learning environment, truly connecting with Oranges and keeping them focused and interested is a special challenge.

I've been grounded so often, I taught myself how to play the guitar. Next week I start a 5 city tour - is that cool or what?

In learning, as in life, they look for hands-on experiences. Ideally, they do not want to be penalized for *attempts* but only for the final product. An easy example is the assembling of a barbecue. Seldom will Oranges even pull out the instructions from the bottom of the box. They will take the parts and start putting them together. Simple as that – through trial and error. Only after they are done, do the instructions make much sense to many Oranges. It becomes a matter of working backwards. First comes the hands-on effort, after which the technical instructions in the manual will make more sense.

Oranges are not keen in too much talk or theory. "Let me at it – let's see what I can do" is their general motto. The music business is full of Orange personalities, and a vast number of them are incredibly talented. Many of them learned to play their first musical instrument in that same manner. Through trial and error, and without formal musical training, but simply by picking up the instrument. Just doing it is always their preferred approach instead of following instructions that teach theory, rules, limitations, or structure.

Oranges look for varied instructions and concrete activities that teach practical material. The Orange mindset evaluates much of their learning in terms of "what's in it for me?" They seek immediate feedback and look for the chance to be the star, center of attention, or winner in whatever the subject. Anything that can be made into a game or a challenge very much appeals to their competitive nature. While that may be possible in workplace seminars, most school systems unfortunately are not able to provide that opportunity.

For many jurisdictions, privacy laws and regulations now don't even allow the publishing of marks or the chance to single out students for recognition! While there may be many valid reasons for this, the downside is that it becomes another area where the education system leaves Orange students behind. Yet it is already the largest "at risk" group in the school system.

Oranges Value
• Hands-on activities and practicality

• Visual and spatial intelligence

• Experimental activities

• Concrete activities for abstract ideas

• A variety of tasks

• The ability to stay active

• Kinesthetic learning

• Challenges and competitions

• The chance to win at something

• The opportunity to be the star or to show off

• Physical challenges

• Minimal rules by staying flexible

• Minimal emphasis on written material and reports

• A fast pace – keep it moving, keep it fresh and interesting

• Experimentation and the chance to try without judgment

• Frequent feedback – but not on experimenting

- Games, races, built-in contests
- The freedom to complete something their way
- Varied displays, change of scenery and frequent breaks

> Orange kids can easily get tired of *fighting the system* as they see it. At some point it becomes a self-fulfilling prophecy. Dropping marks can lead to acting out behavior, generally leading to more pressure to conform and more discipline. This can result in mentally checking out and physically dropping out and quitting.

By all accounts, Henry is one of the best teachers in his secondary school. He is high Gold with Green as his second Color (it is the color combination of large numbers of teachers). His classes consist of over 50 percent Orange students whose mind-set toward rules, deadlines, and being on time is quite the opposite of Henry. Even decades ago, he started to realize that traditional learning styles were not going to reach these kids.

Through trial and error, Henry addressed both those issues in practical and easy ways that made him one of the school's favorite teachers. Through incorporating lots of hands-on exercises and projects and the use of tools, these kids now had a chance to actively contribute in class.

Ways of disciplining Orange students became more of a challenge. The traditional method of sending them to the Principals office had minimal effect on them. In fact, to many of them, it was almost a status symbol amongst their friends.

It became more of a way to show off, rather than one of accepting punishment. Henry's Gold/Green personality also wanted to deal with this challenge himself, without simply passing the problem off to the administration office. This reflected his strong Gold sense of accepting responsibility, and the strength of the Green mindset in looking at the big picture and finding an innovative solution.

But how to deal with the pent-up Orange energy – their need to always be on the move and their lack of proper school discipline? His solution became simple, yet powerful. "Get down and do 20 push-ups!" While his students were horrified at first, it soon became almost a game in his classes. An innovative solution that balanced the need for some kind of discipline with a very Orange opportunity to show off and do something physical. To this day, Henry often runs into students that have long since graduated and have families of their own. Yet some of them will still drop to the ground in the middle of a shopping center years later and excitedly show off that they can still do the 20 push ups. They are still primary Orange, and adults now, but still love to perform and show off.

The Blue Preferences

Many Blues would love to start the workshop or class with a hug if the truth were known. As they are highly intuitive and can readily spot a phony, they will supply quick feedback whether they believe this is actually genuine or not. How sad for Blues that in today's society it may have to be limited to a warm smile, good eye contact, and acknowledging them in a caring verbal manner.

Their strong desire for relationships means that learning is done best in group settings. They seek to make this a group journey involving frequent chances to share and to talk with others. They value opportunities to do much of their work in team activities. Working together and sharing builds their self-esteem and enhances their ability and enjoyment of learning almost anything. Imposed deadlines help them to stay on task, as does the possibility of being separated from their group should they not stay focused. Blues enjoy contributing and helping in their environment. In whatever way that is made possible, they love the chance to be helpful to their team, instructor, and others.

Blues look to see and buy into the big picture outline before dealing in the specific modules or segments. Just learning pieces or sections of modules without that outline is a challenge for them. Most often mentioned is their desire for a fellow Blue instructor that is attuned to their needs and desires and not primarily task-focused. In the school system, frequently some excellent feedback will come from the parents. As Blue kids will likely not stand up for their needs, it will be the parents that will hear their needs at home. With this in mind, it is helpful during training sessions to watch that Blues do not succumb to the wishes of others, or peer pressure, but do get a chance to have their own opinions and input heard.

Blues Value
• A warm and caring instructor
• Any conversational group settings
• Learning from someone attuned to individual needs
• Group work and discussions
• Chance to go off topic to discuss the human aspect
• Frequent verbal positive feedback
• Active listening from others and instructors
• Easy going style with humor
• Positive gestures, smiles and reassurance
• A safe and trusting environment
• Being offered choices instead of demands
• No put-downs, judgments, or intolerance
• Storytelling and sharing time
• Being aware of relationship dynamics in the group
• The chance to help and contribute
• A fair structure with reasonable time-line and deadlines
• Opportunities to build friendships and social interactions
• Making sure everyone is heard and their opinion and input is included

The Gold Preferences
      Overall, Golds look for structure, rules, and a fixed routine in most environments, from the home to their jobs. That desire naturally extends to the education system. Most learning environments are already structured in a Gold manner. They

are normally set up with many clocks, specific and fixed rules, firm deadlines, and an overall organized environment that Golds value. When those structures are not in place, Golds will first focus their energies in an attempt to create them, whenever possible. It is what makes them feel comfortable and allows Golds to then focus on their strength, which is their ability to be task-oriented. They look for proper structure and systems along with clear and detailed instructions. Golds value their ability to stay on track and are frequently turned off by others that get sidetracked, joke around, or go off topic. A big stress for them is not having clearly spelled out instructions. That includes fair discipline and clearly understood methods in which they are graded or measured in a consistent manner.

Do you have any books on how to understand Gold parents or teachers?

Golds seek a logical lesson plan or agenda with distinct steps to completion. Since one of their strengths is to be able to stay on task, they seek checkpoints to validate this and look for progress reports as feedback to measure their progress. In all learning environments, Golds look for extensive handouts and to have research material readily available and organized. They tend to have the same high expectations of their instructor as they do of themselves. Quite frequently, they will be harder on themselves than any teacher or instructor in an effort to do well and with a constant concern about their marks. Their mindset focuses on an overall desire to get the job done before it is time to have fun and relax. Hence, a business-like approach to learning greatly appeals to their orderly nature. They will both exhibit it and look for it in their instructors. Too much fun, non-essentials, or getting sidetracked significantly detracts from their learning experiences. This group has no difficulty staying focused and conforming to acceptable behavior in any environment.

Golds Value

- Staying within time-lines and schedules
- Establishing and following fixed routines and formats
- High expectations for both behavior and academics
- An organized and structured environment
- Quiet time to focus and get the task done
- Individual accomplishments
- Clearly defined expectations, goals, and assignments
- Concrete and specificsteps in material and presentation
- Minimal group work
- Measurable and concrete recognition and rewards
- Understanding the justifications and rationale
- Traditional teaching methods – skills and drills
- Obedience, conformity, and accountability
- Clear goal-setting with their input
- Rewards and recognition for accomplishments
- Inventory of available resources and links
- Being motivated to do well – for self and others
- Non confrontational, very accepting of rules and structure
- Clear, fair, and well known standards
- Consistent measurement of achievements

Chapter 12

Self Esteem and Stress

Webster's dictionary defines self-esteem as holding in high regard, or to set a high value on, admire and respect. Each of the chapters for the four Colors has described their unique strengths and joys in detail. Others cannot build our self-esteem. Bosses, parents, or friends can point someone in the right direction and pave the way, but self-esteem is always derived from within. It grows from what someone does, how they behave, what they do for others – in any number of ways, but always from within. It does not come through verbal affirmations or teaching, but rather through acts and behaviors.

When we live and function each day, week, or longer in ways that feed our joys and strengths, it contributes to building our self-esteem. It grows and grows with each obstacle successfully tackled, with each accomplishment however small that we choose to view as having made a difference, or each time we reach out to touch the lives of others around us.

"Don't undermine your self-worth by comparing yourself with others. It is because we are different that each of us is special."
Nancye Sims

We all strive to function in ways that reinforce this esteem, and to continuously grow in positive ways. Being "in esteem" makes people feel great and creates the feeling of being on top of the world. In our jobs, it translates to a sense that we are not actually working at all, but doing something we love to do – and it shows. It is often a state of mind where nothing will get to us. Fewer things become an annoyance, and obstacles seem somehow much smaller and easy to tackle. The lows are not nearly as low, the attitude is relaxed, and things just seem to get better and better.

In general, having esteem translates to being authentic. It means being and functioning as the person you really are. Blues find it through their meaningful and lasting relationships, their drive to create harmony and touching others with their warmth, caring, and communication skills when they speak from the heart.

For Golds, it is the deep sense of duty and responsibility. They esteem themselves by being of service, as well as through the safety of their strong organizational and planning skills. It is through their desire of functioning within the rules of society and a sense of order, and a general view of life as right or wrong in which they find great satisfaction.

"Nobody really knows how much they can accomplish until they choose to stand up and try."

Greens esteem themselves through the power of knowledge and understanding. One of their primary drives is the constant search for information, improved processes, and a focus on the big picture. They place great value in attempting to understand almost everything around them and seek out opportunities to share their knowledge by teaching others. They value their logical thought process and calm demeanor in the face of pressure situations. Greens understand and rely on their analytical ability, which allows them to deal with complex or intricate problems.

Oranges feel esteemed by being high energy, and by retaining their freedom and fun. At the same time, little pleases Oranges more than having lots of things on the go. They love the thrill of the sale, negotiating anything they can, the chance to think on their feet or direct, hands-on involvement. These are just some of the ways that Oranges can show off their skills and look for the thrill of having each day be different than the day before. They love being the center of attention and want to use their creative talents. This ranges from problem solving to finding practical solutions to almost any challenge or obstacle.

You...
"Never be content with someone else's definition of you.
Instead, define yourself by your own beliefs, your own
truths, your own understanding of who you are, and how
you came to be. And never be content until you are happy
with the unique person you are!"
Author unknown

Measuring Success

Often, success is used as another yardstick in measuring or achieving self-esteem. Not in the material sense, but more through a sense of accomplishment.

There is a significant difference in the yardstick of success for everyone. What is important to each of us has to be separated from those things society, role models, or even our employer tells us is important. The key is not to measure our success against others. Understanding and reconciling these different opinions builds our self-esteem. It is only when we focus on outside views of success – at the expense of our own – that we become unhappy, stressed, and out of esteem.

Knowing and understanding our personality type allows us to uncover our unique strengths and our very own definition of success. It gives us the road map to work toward them in our relationships, home life, and career. Frequently, success is as simple as measuring it in quantitative terms. Making budget, the sales quota, reaching bonus, or completing everything on the day's to-do list are all examples of quantitative ways to measure some form of success.

In most instances, however, it is not that simple. Measuring success is often in the eye of the beholder. A high Blue person can view success as spending a part of their day listening to the needs of someone and knowing they made a difference. Or conversely, they could look at it in terms of "I should have done more," which would certainly never be a self-esteem builder.

For Golds, choosing to measure something as successful is often more difficult. Their general demeanor is one of concern and being very hard on themselves, which creates special challenges. Often Golds need to believe that they consistently give a 100 percent effort to everything they take on. To know they always do the best they possibly can, regardless of the outcome. But the hardest part to accept is letting their best efforts be good enough. When they accept this attitude, it can measurably impact their judgment of success, instead of the Gold thoughts of looking for pitfalls and focusing on the tiny imperfections instead.

Whatever anyone has for a primary Color, their outlook starts with an attitude and continues with a positive judgment of their many accomplishments and small wins each and every day, in so many ways.

Out of Esteem

Out of esteem has a direct connection to being under stress. Just as self-esteem is achieved in different ways, this state is also very different for each group. In fact, one person's esteem often has the opposite effect on others.

For Oranges, a great thrill is being able to multi-task and having a wide range of things on the go. It prevents boredom and creates great variety in their day. To Golds, being given a number of projects in a day often creates the opposite effect. Their esteem is reinforced by the completion of tasks from start to finish. Both of these show quite a different view of a similar day.

Knowledge is power, as any high Green will verify. If we understand how we behave in our actions and words when we are out of esteem, it can often reduce stressful situations before they get out of hand. Seeing and knowing the warning signs in advance leads us to understand ourselves and those close to us. It frequently gives us powerful clues to actions, reactions and behaviors.

Blue Out of Esteem

Out of esteem behavior for Blues exhibits itself in very uncharacteristic ways. At that point, being with others actually becomes a stress. This is quite an admission for any Blue that values their constant interaction with people. It manifests itself when they have given and given and are simply out of energy, much like a car that has run out of gas. Blues seldom remember the powerful lesson that you must take care of yourself before you can take care of others. They start feeling that nobody cares about them, and that they never really do enough. It also becomes a sense of feeling that "I give and give and do all these things and nobody cares about me, or helps me." In this state, they will often become overly emotional and cry for extended periods of time. They have a tendency to bury their own issues by taking care of others, which allows them to avoid having to deal with their own problem or situation. There are just times when overload is reached, it is just too much, and things blow up.

Out of esteem causes them to wonder whether they truly are alone or if anyone loves them for who they really are. Their difficulty in asking for anything for themselves and inability to say no can cause Blues to reach this point. After all, they feel that any show of being selfish means others might not like them anymore. The drive to be liked and included is fundamental to their self-esteem. The Blue depression is brought on because even in this state, they are reluctant to ask for help. When this boils over, it can show itself through anger, which can also lead to yelling or acting out. The out-of-esteem state can create large selfish streaks in them for short periods of time. After having bent and stretched to the wishes of others for so long, it manifests itself as the other extreme of selfishness. In other instances, it can also show itself through very passive behavior or withdrawing altogether.

Green Out of Esteem

Out of esteem behavior for Greens will be noticeable only in subtle ways. The primary Green way is to withdraw further from interacting with others. They become even quieter and *hide* in their minds. They are already very critical and hard on themselves, so being in this state exacerbates it even further. The Green mind goes through waves of second-guessing many decisions they have made. This focus of beating themselves up does not just involve the current problem that has brought this state on. It will involve issues sometimes going back years that they re-live, re-think, and re-analyze something in terms of why it happened, or what they could have done differently. For current projects, this over-analyzing can become a period of paralysis. It often puts them into a state of not making decisions at all. This is not due to any lack of information or time, but because of their out-of-esteem state of second-guessing and freezing on decision making.

Alternately, they can become totally one-tracked and focused exclusively on one issue that consumes their thought process. Greens may also exhibit signs of stubbornness, which can show in their refusal to cooperate with anyone. The most observable outward expression is exhibited through frequent sarcastic and sharp, judgmental comments. Greens have an extensive vocabulary and the gift of words. In this state, it can often become a sharp weapon for them.

Orange Out of Esteem

Our Orange friends seek to stay on a natural high in life. If that cannot be accomplished in constructive ways, they are unfortunately, the largest group of substance abusers. Out of esteem behavior can include alcohol, drugs, or gambling. It may not create the same duration of highs, but in the eyes of some, it is an easy way to achieve it for a while. They can also act out, or behave very rudely. Their normal high physical energy can turn to visible anger that may even erupt into violent behavior. Sometimes it will lead to all out battles with this group. They will break rules and policies on purpose as part of this acting-out behavior. Revenge is also something that goes through the mind of Oranges in this state, with an overwhelming sense of anger and wanting to get even. Their great thrill of making things happen may well turn to paralysis. It is a state where they avoid or delay decisions and become procrastinators. There is one final, regretful behavior. It involves the act of simply quitting or walking away. Whether that is in a relationship or job, Oranges are capable of making a snap decision to simply walk. As the Johnny Paycheck song says, "Take this job and shove it."

Gold Out of Esteem

When Golds reach this point, their general demeanor of being concerned turns even more negative. They will start over planning and over preparing almost everything to the nth degree and will display visible signs of anxiety and worry. One of their general personality traits is that they are very hard on themselves. In this state, that criticism turns outward to include those around them, including verbal criticisms and harsh judgment toward others. Their black or white view becomes even more defined and there is a tendency to become very rigid and strict in their behavior. Golds generally work toward closure and getting things done. However, in this state they are likely to simply quit on something to put the matter behind them, in one way or another. It becomes a "what's the use" or "what's the point trying" type of attitude. This can also extend to trouble in relationships or other difficult positions they may find themselves in. At some point, they just simply want their troubles to be over. If that means quitting, so be it – at least it will mean closure to allow them to move forward.

They can often avoid relying on others and become solo performers. Further signals are signs of fatigue and depression, with Golds often just wishing to hide in bed until this has all passed. Frequently this is brought on as a result of burnout. At those times, Golds just re-live their view of how much they've done for others, the many times they have gone above and beyond the call of duty, and how little recognition or gratitude they actually receive. During this period, they exhibit strong signs of feeling sorry for themselves and seek ways of getting that sympathy from others as well.

"Hurdles are in your life for jumping."
Rev. Sharon Poindexter

The above are designed to be some commonly seen behaviors or warning signs of out of esteem behavior. As every person is unique, these may overlap or manifest themselves in a multitude of other ways. Out of esteem behaviors should act as a warning sign to friends, employers, family, co-workers, and others that things are not going well. It is always best if these signs are identified in their earlier stages, rather than later. At times, it is something that passes quickly, other times it is a state that lingers.

In either event, every person can use a hand and a friend. It is frequently very hard for someone to ask for help. Being a friend, understanding, caring, and listening are always of great value in these types of situations. In addition, there are numerous valuable self-help books that may be of assistance. When out of esteem behavior persists or deepens, making the effort to visit with a professional is another excellent tool to use sooner, rather than later. They are a great source of specific, focused, and often invaluable information.

Chapter 13

Gifts and Presents

*"My husband gave me a tire pump for my birthday.
Does that mean he really cares about me being
stranded somewhere, or does he just not want
me to bother him when I am?"*

That is probably not the first thing anyone should hear right after the words "thank you." Webster's defines a gift not only as a present, but also as "a special ability." How very true and appropriate that both fall under the same definition. To buy a special gift for someone is often a challenge, but it comes with great rewards when it is done well.

Nothing ever replaces knowing someone's favorite sport, author, music style, or hobby when looking for that perfect present. Something that the recipient will honestly appreciate, value and enjoy. While this chapter does not replace that knowledge, there are some basic common themes and ideas valued by each group. Often, it is even harder than the overall male-female gift giving challenge. Without ruling out a practical gift, lawn mowers tend not to be a good idea for any lady.

"For gifts that people really want and might actually use."
Office Max Advertisement

For Golds

When buying gifts for Golds, keep in mind their desire for practicality. Both in terms of the type of gift and the amount of money spent on it. They do not look for the flashy or extravagant. "Is the gift useful" and "is it good quality" are two good questions to ask. Will they recognize that it has been thoughtfully picked just for them, and is it good value for the money, are two more questions to remember before going shopping. For Golds, this does not generally include gift certificates. In their judgment, that is not an appropriate gift, and they frequently view it as a cop-out.

Golds also place great value on the actual birthday or anniversary day, which means the exact day. Hearing that "we'll just celebrate on the weekend instead" or "I'll have your present when I see you Wednesday" is not appropriate for Golds. Their general mindset of black or white means the specific day should be recognized, and not carried-over over to the weekend, or another convenient date.

Some Gift Ideas

Appointment books

Books on finance, investing or time-management

Calendar (targeted to their hobbies or likes)

Classy pen sets

Clothing – conservative & good quality

Day-timers

Good quality picture frame

Palm pilot (ensure they are comfortable with it
   or they will not use it)

Personalized stationary or note paper

Quality desk accessories

Research for their family tree

Subscription to financial or news magazine

Watch or clock

No section for Golds would be complete without some small feedback on their occasional concept of gift giving. It might not be fair to single out Golds, but it is probably accurate to say that many of them can benefit from some lateral thinking and variety approach to this subject.

A frequent challenge is the idea that not all gifts need to be practical. The Gold value for organization, planning, and practicality often extends to their ideas of great gifts. Yes, office supply stores can be great places to find gifts for this group. They are not often the same places that other groups want their presents to come from. It is important for Golds not to judge gifts on a practicality scale, and to avoid looking first at the price tag before deciding.

That's Fernando. He's my acting coach. I'm going to need some help reacting to the presents I get for my birthday tomorrow.

For Blues

Blues do not seek to be the center of attention for any celebration or party. As Blues are very unselfish, they will generally tell the world that they don't want to make a fuss and that any celebration is not really necessary. Nothing could be further from the truth. It is simply a high Blue not wanting to appear selfish, or asking anything for themselves. Inside, they love and thrive on others noticing them and showing they are valued and cared about by recognizing their special occasion. Blues will be on top of the world and feeling hugely special, while claiming it wasn't necessary at all.

"Teach others what you value and look for in gifts."

To Blues it is extra special when a gift is picked just for them. Anything they would not buy or do for themselves can be the perfect gift. It may be as simple as getting them an afternoon off work, as an example. It should be remembered that their unselfishness means others in their lives had best keep track of their special dates as the Blues will not let it be known. They will, however, be quite hurt if it is forgotten or missed by their friends or coworkers.

Some Gift Ideas

Books with theme of romance, possibilities,
   or self-improvement

Candles or candle holders

Clothing if it's soft to the touch (i.e. fleece)

Decorated picture frames

Desk size mini waterfall

Diary or journal

Dinner party with friends

Family pictures or album

Fresh flowers

Handmade or meaningful card

Romantic dinner

Romantic video or DVD

Self improvement course or seminar

Software reminder program for birthdays/anniversaries

Spa or massage gift certificate

Special writing paper

Warm card signed by everyone from the office

Weekend get-away

"If nothing else, be a great receiver.
Make a big deal out of the gifts
that are appropriate and really treasured."

For Greens

Greens value knowledge and learning. Understanding this makes shopping for the Green gift a much easier task. They seek to give and receive the perfect present. A Green will often go shopping for hours with that goal. At the end of it, they may well come away with a present that is perfect to them, if not for the person they are shopping for. Or frequently, they may well purchase a gift certificate After all, if a gift certificate is not the best present, it is certainly close. It allows the recipient to find the ideal present for themselves. To the Green mind, what could be better – what could be more logical? Others are often disappointed to *only* receive a gift certificate, however in the mind of a Green, it is the most logical way to get the gift they really wish for. They have spent hours shopping and making their best effort to find the appropriate gift and others don't often realize how much thought has gone into the presents they choose.

Some Gift Ideas

Books if they are: Non-fiction, reference type, knowledge
or *make you think* type

Bookstore gift certificate

Computer accessories – software or magazine

Hi-tech stuff – almost anything

Home made wine kit

Instrumental or classical music tape or CD

Puzzles

Science fiction or mystery video or DVD

Something from a science store

Subscription to scientific magazine or National Geographic

For Oranges

Fun and freedom are the key motivators for Oranges. They enjoy the latest, greatest things and thrive on action. A great celebration for Oranges is to receive, or to help create a great surprise of any kind. As a result, they also love it when others make them the "star of the show" on their birthday or anniversary, through any number of unique and attention-getting ways. When Oranges celebrate an event, it is always a party. That usually means lots of friends, a great time, and a very late night. Oranges do not think anything of reminding everyone they see for weeks before that their birthday, anniversary, or a special event is coming up.

They love being the center of attention and this is another reason to make it so. Unless it is a surprise party, Oranges like to be involved in deciding what to do. It is their special day, after all. Often, their biggest concern is making sure the celebration does not turn out to be a drag. If another Orange is in charge of the planning, they will be much more willing to allow someone else to take control. When it comes to actually finding presents for Oranges, they are not much interested in practical gifts. The biggest factors include making sure the gift draws attention or is very unique or hard to find. If it involves a party, for them to get noticed makes it extra special. Whether that's being on the marquis at the football game or an announcement on the P.A. system, it will be a welcome surprise sure to delight and thrill them.

Some Gift Ideas
A funny or wild card
A mention on the radio
Billboard, lawn sign, or ad in the newspaper
Clothes – flashy or trendy
Fitness club membership or sports equipment
Money
MP3, or DVD player, or Walkman
Night on the town with limousine ride
VIP pass to a cool nightclub
Restaurant gift certificate
Something unique, rare, or hard to find
Surprise party or weekend get-away
Tickets to a sporting event or show
Upbeat music CD or DVD

When it comes to buying gifts themselves, these are definitely the largest group of last minute shoppers. Shopping the day before Christmas is frequently referred to by merchants as *boys day out*. While last minute shopping is an often seen male characteristic, it is actually a strong Orange trait. Procrastination and last minute scrambling are not unusual for this group. The downside to that style of shopping is that there is little opportunity to search for the perfect present.

Oranges tend to be destination shoppers in any event. Wandering through stores or malls with no other purpose than window-shopping, is hardly their idea of a good time. The challenge for this group is to prepare a mental list of great presents in advance of hitting the stores. The alternate scenario is to make the effort to buy presents throughout the year. But the downside to accumulating presents is their challenge to keep them hidden away and to fight the desire of sharing them immediately.

Chapter 14

The Last Word

Notes to each other, and things the world should know:

Golds to certain box stores: "I didn't schedule 15 minutes for shopping to be in the lineup for 42 minutes."

Greens to all sales clerks: "Leave me alone – please! I'll let you know if I need you. Please stay away or I will."

Blues to the world: "When we ask how you are, we really do want to know. Is it so hard to give us a real answer? It's OK if it is an answer longer than 'fine'".

Greens to most advertisers: "Stop saying: I'm *saving* to shop at your store. When I spend money I don't save it – I might be getting a discount, but I'm SPENDING not SAVING and there is a difference."

Oranges to bank machine customers: "Please keep it to 40 transactions or less, and move on. I'm stuck behind you, always out of money and have a life to get back to, you know."

Orange/Green to others: "Hey after 16 hours of action, problem solving and multi-tasking I turn totally anti-social. Just so you're warned, there is an end in sight for me to re-charge."

Golds to certain grocery chains: "When I buy toast and milk do NOT ask me if I need help to the car with that – honest!"

Oranges to Golds: "What are you talking about? They ask that? Gee, I'm long gone by then, I never knew."

Oranges to all others: "We ask you quite often if you want to come along, or do something. You're not excluded; it's just that it takes you too long to decide. We're still going, with our without you. You just need to decide a little faster to keep up."

Greens & Golds to Blues: "Don't get your feelings hurt when we walk past you without saying 'hello'. Our mind is definitely somewhere else and it's nothing you've done, honest!"

Oranges to others in the house: "Yes, as a matter of fact, I do own the remote control Sit back and watch – it's not hard to catch two or three shows at the same time and never see a commercial all night."

Golds, Blues & Greens to car salesmen: "Don't ask me if I'm buying today. It assures that I won't be buying today or ever from you!"

Oranges & Golds to many businesses: "Please figure out how to make your voice mail system work a lot quicker. Press 6, then 4, then star, then 0 is a sure-fire way to make us hang up. Who has time for that?"

Green boss to all staff: "I distinctly remember telling you last year that you're doing a good job. How often do I have to repeat myself?"

Greens to others: "Yes, sarcasm is a acceptable form of humor – honestly."

Golds & Oranges to anyone ahead of them in a line-up: "Please dig out your change before you get to the front of the line. I'd like to get out of the store today too. It is NOT mandatory that you have exact change to pay with."

Oranges to others: "Forget sending me long e-mails. I avoid using a computer as much as possible after work. If you want to talk – give me a call. Better yet, catch me in person."

Blues and Oranges to Golds: "Yes, we sometimes have a problem being on time for you. But have you ever noticed that people who are late are jollier than those who had to wait? It is because of you that most of us have our clocks set ahead in the first place"

Orange/Blues to other Oranges: "Hey cut me some slack. I know that I'm competitive, but not at the expense of hurting others."

Greens to all others: "Hello - remember us? Stop wondering about things and ask us We can figure it out and fix things for you, use your head."

Golds to Post-it-Notes inventor: "Thank you, thank you, thank you – I can't live without them anymore."

Blues to Greens: "Don't fix – just listen when we talk to you. We just want to be heard and not have you fix our problems."

Once Upon a Time

Last, but not least a story to always remind us to spend more time looking for what we have in common than looking to our differences:

Once upon a time the colors of the world started to quarrel. All claimed that they were the best, the most important, the most useful.

Green said: "Clearly I am the most important. I am the sign of life and of hope. I was chosen for grass, trees and leaves. Without me, all animals would die. Look over the countryside and you will see that I am in the majority."

Blue retorted: "You only think about the earth, but consider the sky and the sea. It is the water that is the basis of life and drawn up by the clouds from the deep sea. The sky gives space and peace and serenity. Without my peace, you would all be nothing."

Yellow chuckled: "You are all so serious. I bring happiness and warmth into the world. The sun is yellow, the moon is yellow, and the stars are yellow. Every time you look at a sunflower, the whole world starts to smile. Without me there would be no joy."

Orange started next to blow her trumpet: "I am the color of health and strength. I may be scarce, but I am precious for I serve the needs of human life. I carry the most important vitamins. Think of carrots, pumpkins, oranges, mangoes, and papayas. I don't hang around all the time, but when I fill the sky at sunrise or sunset, my beauty is so striking that no one gives another thought to any of you."

And so the colors went on boasting, each convinced of his, or her, own superiority. Their quarreling became louder and louder. Suddenly there was a startling flash of bright lightening, and thunder rolled and boomed. Rain started to pour down relentlessly. The colors crouched down in fear, drawing close to one another for comfort.

In the midst of the clamor, rain began to speak: "You foolish colors, fighting amongst yourselves, each trying to dominate the rest. Don't you know that you were each made for a special purpose, unique and different? Join hands with one another and come to me."

Doing as they were told, the colors united and joined hands. The rain continued: "From now on, when it rains, each of you will stretch across the sky in a great bow of color as a reminder that you can all live in peace. So whenever a good rain washes the world, and a Rainbow appears in the sky let us remember to appreciate one another."

A Note From the Author

For those of you who have already attended a seminar, you have seen first-hand the vast difference between reading the book and *living* the training. It brings the material to life in three-dimensional ways with tools that last a lifetime. More than 500,000 people each year participate in seminars to learn the powerful and practical lessons of understanding themselves and others. I would invite you to make that a goal in your life and with your team for this coming year.

Just imagine the positive changes if everyone simply understood us a little better, with the tools and knowledge to *speak our language*, celebrate our differences, and value us just the way we are.

If you have a short story of a personal triumph using your newfound understanding, please contact me. Hopefully you will care enough to share it with others. In addition, if you are aware of the individuals to give credit to for any "author unknown" quotes, please let me know.

George J. Boelcke, F.C.I.

You can contact me through:
george@vantageseminars.com
or my web site at: www.vantageseminars.com

George Boelcke is President of Vantage Consulting.

He has over 25 years of 'real world' management and ownership experience in the retail, finance, fitness and automotive industries.

From private groups to schools, corporations of all sizes, to conventions, he facilitates seminars on personality types, team building, sales, marketing and relationships throughout North America and is recognized as having one of the most extensive web sites on creating understanding of personality types and Colors at:www.vantageseminars.com

The Colors Self-Assessment

Score each group of words, for all eight questions, on a scale of:

        4 – which is the most like you

        3 – which is quite a bit like you

        2 – which is a little bit like you

        1 – which is the least like you

(Each question can have only one score of 1, one 2, one 3 and one 4)

1. a) ____ compassion, sharing, sympathetic

   b) ____ duty, detailed, traditions

   c) ____ verbal, risk-taker, promoter

   d) ____ rational, knowledge, visionary

2. a) ____ feelings, meaningful, cooperation

   b) ____ conservative, reliable, stability

   c) ____ spontaneous, generous, action

   d) ____ credibility, focused, probing

3. a) ____ authentic, encouraging, spiritual

   b) ____ devoted, cautious, status-quo

   c) ____ surprises, freedom, short-cuts

   d) ____ inventive, principled, competence

4. a) ____ unique, sensitive, peace-maker

   b) ____ steady, planning, loyal

   c) ____ open-minded, playful, hands-on

   d) ____ curious, determined, rational

5. a) ____ tender, involved, connecting
   b) ____ lists, procedural, responsible
   c) ____ competitive, outgoing, direct
   d) ____ exploring, skeptical, complex

6. a) ____ devoted, caring, self-improvement
   b) ____ dependable, structured, belonging
   c) ____ flexible, daring, persuasive
   d) ____ independent, perfectionist, reserved

7. a) ____ intuition, sharing, positive
   b) ____ orderly, honor, rule-follower
   c) ____ immediate, skillful, active
   d) ____ theoretical, calm & cool, learning

8. a) ____ affectionate, accommodating, harmony
   b) ____ private, serious, moral
   c) ____ networking, adventure, winning
   d) ____ analytical, logical, improving

Your total score for:

a) Blue ____ b) Gold ____ c) Orange ____ d) Green ____

(The total of your four scores will equal 80)

Order Form

#	Title	Investment per	Total amount
_____	Colorful Personalities – Discover Your Personality Type Through the Power of Colors	US: $ 14.95 CAN: $19.95	_____
_____	Colorful Personalities – Audio CD	US: $ 14.95 CAN: $19.95	_____
_____	The Colors of Leadership and Management booklet	US: $ 4.90 CAN: $ 5.95	_____
_____	The Colors of Parent and Child Dynamics booklet	US: $ 4.90 CAN: $ 5.95	_____
_____	The Colors of Sales and Customers booklet	US: $ 4.90 CAN: $ 5.95	_____
_____	The Colors of Relationships booklet	US: $ 4.90 CAN: $ 5.95	_____
_____	Any four booklets package	US: $ 14.95 CAN: $19.95	_____
_____	It's Your Money! Tools, tips and tricks to borrow smarter & pay it off quicker	US: $ 14.95 CAN: $19.95	_____
	Sales Tax or GST		**no charge**
	Postage (flat amount)		**$ 4.00**
	Total amount:		_____

Payment and mailing information:

Name: _____

Address: _____

City: _____ State/Prov: _____ Zip/PC: _____

E-mail: _____

Payment enclosed by: _____check _____cash _____money order, or

Visa/MC: _____/_____/_____/_____ Expiry date:____/____

Order by: Fax: (780) 432 5613   Phone: 866 896 6609
E-mail: sales @ vantageseminars.com
Mail: U.S.: 1183 - 14781 Memorial Dr., Houston, TX 77079
Canada: Box 4080 Edmonton, AB, T6E 4S8